T0354493

Owning and Sowing
Seeds of Peace

Owning and Sowing Seeds of Peace

An Autobiographical Perspective

Francis S. Nicol

OWNING AND SOWING SEEDS OF PEACE
AN AUTOBIOGRAPHICAL PERSPECTIVE

Scripture quotations marked KJV are from the Holy Bible, King James Version (Authorized Version). First published in 1611. Quoted from the KJV Classic Reference Bible, Copyright © 1983 by The Zondervan Corporation.

iUniverse books may be ordered through booksellers or by contacting:

iUniverse
1663 Liberty Drive
Bloomington, IN 47403
www.iuniverse.com
1-800-Authors (1-800-288-4677)

ISBN: 978-1-5320-7163-8 (sc)
ISBN: 978-1-5320-7164-5 (e)

Library of Congress Control Number: 2019903566

Print information available on the last page.

iUniverse rev. date: 12/26/2019

Contents

Francis Nicol has presented a view of peace that draws the reader to consciousness of its various forms and its importance in our time. He uses knowledge of these forms to assess their impact on his life. It is a unique approach to the writing of his autobiography. Within his model of peace, Dr. Nicol weaves around his life, a network of strands that has shielded his life from the turmoil of the environments through and within which he has moved, amid the obstacles and challenges he encountered on his way to self-actualization. This he shows by tracing his development from early childhood to adult life in the country of his birth, to his achievement of the various accolades that he has proudly won abroad. The book displays the author's gift of inquiry, as he examines the concept of peace in some known religions. In this way, he leads the reader through his understanding of peace and its intrinsic quality for him. He stresses in this process the importance of having not only the desire but the means of creating and preserving that peace in the individual as well as globally.

Owning and Sowing Seeds of Peace demonstrates Dr. Nicol's capability as an accomplished researcher to tell a life story in an absorbing form. He shows himself clearly as a gifted storyteller. He uses a style that is engaging, flowery, and flowing. Reading through this book is a treat not to be missed. Here, the reader is submerged in a story told effortlessly in a sequence of revealing and entertaining events. I heartily recommend it for literary enrichment and personal inspiration.

—Prof. Dr. Kosonike Koso-Thomas

An accomplished civil engineer, educator, writer, artist, and author of several books, Dr. Kosonike Koso-Thomas was Vice Chancellor of the University of Sierra Leone.

Acknowledgments

As long as I live, I will relish the instructions, the illuminating moral precepts, and the empowering examples of my parents, Lily and Edward Nicol. I extol the blazing trails they inherited from their parents (particularly Mama Yo and Grandpa Tommy), which they, in turn, transmitted to me and bequeathed to posterity. I thank them for the zeal with which they furnished light and courage to me. I also thank them for their generous gifts of love, as well as their sundry resources that enabled me to translate those gifts into tangible and shimmering outcomes. To my older siblings—Princess, Prince, Oangissi, and Wachuku—I say thank you for having enriched my experiences and enhanced my efforts to extract meaning from a constantly changing world.

My appreciation and gratitude go to Dr. Yinka and Dr. Kosonike Koso-Thomas for the stimulating discussions, glowing inspiration, wise counsel, and enlightened exchanges from which I learned and benefited enormously. My thanks also go to Mrs. Agatha Jalloh for the invaluable advice and inestimable support she consistently provided during my writing of this book. Likewise, many thanks go to an outstanding mixed pool of manuscript reviewers, esteemed friends, and colleagues—Dr. Hilda Dunkwu, Dr. Willet Wright, Mrs. Daphne Marke, and Messieurs Kenneth Kromanty and Foday Koroma—who, in varied ways, helped to refresh my memory, refine my conviction, and sharpen my perspectives, while verifying compliance with acceptable literary prescriptions.

To all those persons, named and unnamed, with whom I interacted meaningfully, from whom I learned, and whose literary product enriched me, I express my deep and genuine gratitude. I trust that the confidence invested in the content and quality of my work has not been misplaced.

Chapter 1

Contextualizing the Different Shades of Peace

> Unless men increase in wisdom as much as in knowledge, increase of knowledge will be increase of sorrow.
>
> —Bertrand Russell

Introduction

Throughout my numberless classroom hours as a student, teacher, university professor, and instructional leader or observer, and despite my expansive foreign travels and sojourn, a satisfactory understanding of the concept of peace consistently eluded me. Not even the assumed erudition associated with the acquisition of six university credentials from four institutions of higher learning on three continents would prove adequate to master the attainment of peace. Likewise, neither my almost interminable interface with diverse peoples and their cultures nor my perpetual striving for intellectual refinement sufficiently quenched my thirst for a peace-inducing understanding of the concept. Drawing from my unique background, education, and experience, the topic begged not only for a serious investigation but also for one with me as the primary investigative tool.

From the cradle to the grave, our lives are impacted by our understanding, perception, and embracing of peace. At birth, humans usher in the cyclical challenges associated with restoring, attaining, and maintaining peace. We frequently mention the peaceful disposition of the newborn babe, while in almost the same breath, we commit the soul of the departed to rest in perpetual peace. Thus, peace is manifest at birth and is invoked perpetually even after death. By the same token, we conjure different shades of peace in our hopes, wishes, and aspirations for ourselves and our loved ones. The pervasive absence of peace, the need for peace, the search for strategies to attain it, or the nuanced interpretation of peace has remained confounding and perplexing. More important, the peaks and valleys in my personal life compelled me to invest countless hours on its contemplation. Therefore, I explore the concept and conduct this investigation against the backdrop of my experiences and courtship with peace.

This book is an attempt to seek (and not to present) answers to some of the baffling questions and experiences associated with what constitutes peace, how I venture to achieve it, and its value to the individual and society. I examine varied constructs of peace at various points where they intersect with life-changing events and experiences in my life. As a product of the people with whom I have interacted and of the books and other literary artifacts that have shaped me, I weave various strands and shades of peace into the experiential mosaic of my biography. Thus, *Owning and Sowing Seeds of Peace* is the medium I have conscientiously chosen to probe into the various attributes of peace. Through the lenses of my personal experiences and relevant literature, I attempt to examine, define, and react to the emergent phenomenon of peace.

The first of five chapters of this book describes the context in which the investigation of peace evolves. In this endeavor, I assume the posture of the investigator as well as the primary instrument of the investigation. Chapter 1 furnishes the context in which I present a variety of perspectives gleaned from research, as well as my experiences in specified settings. I elucidate on some generic sources of turmoil that threaten to obscure or disrupt the cultivation of peace. Additionally, the chapter furnishes the reader with a rationale and purpose of the investigation, the significance, and the methods of analysis.

Chapter 2 reviews the prominent literature that I have deemed relevant to the investigation. This chapter contextualizes the construct of peace within the framework of organized religions. Three major world religions—Christianity, Islam, and Buddhism—are referenced, and they feature outstandingly in constructing a template for examining the literature that relates to the spiritual dimensions of peace.

Chapter 3 delves into the ubiquity and the major triggers of turmoil. In this chapter, I examine the various manifestations of turmoil and the contrasting influence of peace. My personal experiences, readings, and research in relevant fields provide the context for analysis, interpretation, and content presentation.

Chapter 4 offers an expanded narrative and focus on life-changing events that have tested and shaped my outlook on life. The chapter contains some practical methods, requisite conditions, and strategies that facilitate attaining and maintaining peace. Three prerequisite orientations and conditions for the attainment, restoration, and maintenance of peace (i.e., guiding principles, life-changing experiences, and a maintenance culture of peace) are introduced and discussed. My personal experience, coupled with the relevant literature, provides the basis for my assertions as well as the knowledge base from which recommendations and suggestions are proffered. In this chapter, my dominant intention is to use my personal experiences as a raison d'être and justification for recommending alternatives to turmoil.

Chapter 5 provisionally brings to a conclusion the inconclusive. The chapter presents the closing remarks and recommended strategies for acquiring and assimilating practices that advance the attainment and restoration of peace.

Though it has an autobiographical tilt, this text can serve the reading interests of readers of biographies, religious/Christian life, Diaspora, or inspirational writings. I am also amply convinced that it can augment a reading list for advanced secondary- or tertiary-level studies in English literature and the social or behavioral sciences.

The First Seeds

My quest for understanding and framing the concept of peace emerged from the confluence of life-shaping events and experiences in two dissimilar village communities in the British colonial enclave of Sierra Leone. Throughout my formative years, the villages of Waterloo and Lumley, which edged the Western Peninsula of Sierra Leone, offered two distinct models of a serene and pacific interface with nature. Those boyhood days lent themselves to experiences that were contemporaneously acquired in those two rural settings in roughly equal numbers and intensity. In addition to being a Mecca for peaceful social retreats on weekends, the communities of Lumley and Waterloo conjured an atmosphere of peace and tranquility among their inhabitants, as well as among their sundry admirers and visitors.

During those hardy days (in the 1950s and '60s) which forecast the end of the colonial era in Sierra Leone, Lumley was fondly called *Pa Sanday*. This name evinced marked endearment for the courage and selflessness of the legendary Pa Sandy, after whom the village was named. The expanse of sandy beaches and the varied aquatic resources of the Atlantic attracted a variety of inhabitants and sustained the economically thriving village community of Pa Sanday.

Waterloo, being the historically renowned peaceful retreat and final resting place of soldiers returning from England in the early nineteenth century, was a testament to their exceptional military gallantry during the Battle of Waterloo. Over time, the village of Waterloo evolved as a tranquil retreat and the logical weekend destination for hundreds of holidaymakers, civil servants, and private citizens and their families.

From my frail boyhood recollections at Pa Sanday, where the peaceful melody of the waves often paired with the soothing breeze from the Atlantic Ocean, my interest in the phenomenon of peace mushroomed. Each step on the sandy, meandering trail of the shoreline provided an additional opportunity for the emergence of a new dimension of my then-native notion of peace. With unabashed zeal, I persisted in yearning for the diurnal and serene early-morning walk along Lumley Beach in the company of my father, Edward Nicol. During those strolls, he wasted no opportunity to explain, describe, and discuss lessons of the lore, bordering on Christian values; the natural sciences; or morality. As the days, weeks, months, and years of trailing the seashore yielded increased footprints on the sand, so did my esteem and appreciation for my father's sagacity and affection for me mount. With energy fueled by my youthful ambition to discover and master the bounteous content of Mother Earth, each morning exercise provided one more opportunity to explore my environment and forge explanations for almost everything perceived in it. The sight, sound, feel, and smell of the Atlantic Ocean deceptively lulled me to the conviction that peace was a natural consequence and derivative of a trip to the beach. In my puerile outlook, peace appeared to be the resultant atmosphere and ambiance that the early-morning walk evoked. My mind's eye perceived the beach as a much-needed external source and primary determinant of peace. Ensuing infantile thoughts reinforced the fallacy that, being an extraction from our environment, peace was exclusively the product of environmental factors.

A secondary competing notion of peace emerged from the daily Nicol family morning devotion, which closely followed the promenade on the beach. The family morning devotion was characterized by a re-strengthening of family bonds, a reaffirmation of our faith in God, and the surrendering of the intricate details of our existences to divine will. In the daily scheme of family duties and household chores, the early-morning family devotion assumed a position of importance that was second to none. I knew at an early age that no excuse was good enough to exempt any human occupant of the Nicol household from participating in the morning devotion. Though an inescapable obligation, taking part in the early-morning family devotion was one of my infant fancies. It accorded the first opportunity of the day for each family member to meet and greet, as we joined in the family service of prayer and thanksgiving to our heavenly Father. My mother, who, beyond any doubt, was the spiritual leader of the family, would share the handwritten order of service and advise each participant of his or her assigned role. As for my father, his permanent role of selecting the musical tunes and playing the organ during the devotion was executed with impeccable regularity and assiduity. The other roles—relating to passing out the hymnals, locating the passages of scripture, reading the scripture, and audibly leading the prayer line—were all assigned by my mother, whom we dotingly called Aunty Lily. Aunty Lily was the name bestowed on her by the scores of nieces, nephews, and relatives who had been proud beneficiaries of the strict and nurturing upbringing for which the Nicol household was renowned.

The daily family devotion was instrumental in reaffirming our faith in God, deepening our understanding of God, engaging our spirituality through praise and worship, and strengthening the cords of propinquity. It provided a daily medium through which the spiritual attributes of a peaceful existence were divulged and internalized. That spiritual exercise embodied protocols, rituals, and practices that were meant to establish and maintain communication with our God. The reading, explication, and interpretation of the scriptures; the offering of prayers; and the singing of hymns and canticles were intended and designed for the cultivation and maintenance of peace through spiritual intercourse. Unlike the daily evening bedtime prayers that were meant to thank God for His guidance during the day and for His anticipated protection through the night, the morning devotion set the tone for divine intervention throughout the day. The morning devotion was, therefore, an effective tool for establishing peace with oneself, peace with one's physical and social surroundings, as well as peace with God.

For a while, my devotion-related assignments as the youngest of five children in the union of Edward and Lily Nicol were limited to passing out the hymnals and being ever ready to say a prayer, if and when called upon. Though being noticeably active in the daily devotion, I was shielded from the surfeit of physically or mentally demanding domestic chores. That privileged status endured until I entered standard one (or grade three). The period thereafter marked the beginning of my active participation in the school choir (where my father was the headmaster, or principal) as well as in the church choir (where he was also the church organist and musicologist). My active involvement in these two choral activities broadened my understanding of the scriptures and strengthened my spirituality. Through both, common sense promptly advised me that I could not escape the uncompromisingly strict disciplinary code of my father. I grudgingly accepted the dreaded reality that I had to endure the unfortunate obligation of attending the same school in which my father was the headmaster.

I, therefore, strove to maintain the delicate balance between the demands and expectations of my parents and those of my older siblings. In that process, I sought to enjoy the best of both worlds throughout the period preceding my seventh birthday. With an exaggerated sense of personal freedom, I occasionally connived with my older siblings' relative waywardness. To hang out with them, particularly after dusk, or to engage in any of the so-called adult activities was considered cool. With silky smoothness, I would select the convenient moment to gravitate to my parents for affection, protection, and sustenance. In return, my parents boldly and unequivocally communicated their expectations of my total compliance with the rules and regulations that would keep our family unit peaceful and functional. Competently negotiating those options afforded me the appropriate balance between the two counterpoising forces. For me, then, I clung to the apparent reality that the major sources of peace were the serenity of the beach, closely knit family ties, and meaningful union with other humans and, above all, with our heavenly Father. I developed a keen sense of moderation and a unique understanding of the act of balancing compensation. In scope and profundity, the dominant perspective on peace at this stage of my human interaction mirrored the pedantic notion of "peace of mind." The concept of peace was limited to a state of mind that was triggered and dictated by specific external stimuli. It was far from being a lifestyle.

Allied to that notion of peace were practical lessons on the enduring strength of kindness, service to others, and selfless acts of love. Nothing illustrated this construct of peace as vividly as the daily events at the Pike Street Soja Tong abode of my maternal grandmother. Formally, she was Mary Renner. Lovingly, we called her Mama Yo. *Mama Yo* was the original plea of distress, or "Rescue me." This plea was uttered by one of her young grandnephews, whose soccer-induced sores provoked the kind but merciless attention of Mama Yo. She would painstakingly clean and lovingly treat every visible sore that resulted from our evening soccer matches. The pronouncement of the words *Mama Yo* was a plea for mercy during the painful cleaning and disinfecting of his soccer-induced sores. Mama Yo's kind care and nurturing conveyed the depth of her affection for us, her priceless tender care, and her indiscriminate commitment to the well-being of all the children in her custody. Her acutely kind attention also signaled to us that our bodies were not only delicate but also valued. Therefore, each of us should treat his or hers as such. Her efforts nudged us to the reality that the proper maintenance of our physical bodies was integral to our well-being and quest for peace.

Likewise, not even her hundred-plus years of vibrant life could dilute her zeal to prepare a daily evening meal for her host of grandchildren. The evening meal rendered her residence the natural meeting place of almost all the grandchildren on holiday. Each of our places at Grandma's dinner table was always assured, as long as we upheld Grandma's three cardinal rules, which she enforced with inviolable rigidity: (1) we must be of good report; (2) we must pray before eating; and (3) we must not talk while eating. With predictable regularity, each of us complied. Every day, each of us would enter Mama Yo's pantry to identify his or her special color-coded dish that contained the day's delicacy from Grandma's kitchen. Mama Yo's Sierra Leonean delicacies, particularly her crane-crane sauce which paired uniquely well with foofoo, scrumptiously spelled magic. Her crane-crane sauce stood tall even among her dynamite sawa-sawa (sorrel sauce), dried okra, or bitter-leaf sauce. In addition to her culinary expertise, Mama Yo ably managed her other social and family engagements with flawless regularity. She capably performed her household chores as well as her duties as the church mother and spiritual leader of St. Mark's Church, Waterloo.

A common belief among the grandchildren was that Mama Yo knew everything, and whatever she touched would literally turn gold. Even at the age of 103, her memory was as impressively dependable as her mind was acutely sound. She would tell us about our ancestral ties; describe present family connections; narrate folklore and Waterloo church history;

establish when and how certain family-owned landed properties were acquired; and describe sundry issues relating to the Word and the world. I entertained no doubt that she was God's gift to us and to humanity. The lessons she taught us were memorable, her generosity exemplary, and her faith in God unflinching; her proclivity for righteousness was irreproachable. To this day, life has offered me no better exemplar of righteousness, compassion, and love than Mama Yo. Going to Waterloo on weekends or during school holidays was a treat to which my siblings and I looked forward. To be away from school was, in itself, a gift. Traveling to Waterloo to spend the holidays was undoubtedly among the most exciting events of the year. Above all, spending time with Grandma was peace and happiness personified. In human terms, Mama Yo's lifestyle was my purest model of peace.

My brothers (Prince, David, Wachuku) and I would stringently count the number of days left in the school term. My sister, Princess, being the oldest of the five of us, exercised greater flexibility in deciding when she was to be picked up from her college hostel at Tower Hill. With great expectation, all of us would long for the holidays, when the family would temporarily relocate from Lumley to Waterloo to spend the Easter, rainy season, or Christmas holidays. Paid movers would assist us in the tedious task of moving all valuable goods, including domesticated animals and pets, from one end of the Western Area Peninsula to the other. As children, we found the task slovenly and tedious but abundantly rewarding.

Among the highlights of our holiday stay at Waterloo was the all-day monthly church cleaning on the fourth Saturday of the month. I engaged in the church-cleaning task with great expectancy and joy, nursing the pride that St. Mark's Countess of Huntingdon Church, Waterloo, was highly considered among the oldest and most beautiful churches in Waterloo. As a result, dusting the antique church furniture and cleaning the elegant interior of the building required great attention to detail. The building was not only adorned with delicate metallic fixtures but also generously decorated with ornate architectural designs. The church-cleaning chores ranked second in childhood exhilaration only to the daily afternoon visit to Mama Yo. Both events offered countless opportunities for us to renew friendships and ties with relatives, friends, and other holidaymakers.

In addition to providing an outlet for social interaction, the corporate church-cleaning exercise obliged me to think deeply about my relationship with God, as well as my service to the community of humans. For me, those childhood days were not only exciting and peaceful but also pregnant with social and personal possibilities. Making friends and maintaining friendship proved profoundly rewarding. Mama Yo and other elders of the church exhibited great excitement in working with the children and treating them to snacks. As a child, I extracted immense pleasure from sharing or exchanging snacks with friends and family members. The peace and love shown in our corporate conduct mirrored the tranquil demeanor and generosity of Mama Yo and my parents. As children, we exhibited a penchant for love and service to others in our thoughts, words, and actions.

Those experiences also contrasted well with the nonhuman events associated with the awe-inspiring vastness and serenity of Lumley Beach. In the deep corner of my mind, a path to peace was effectively constructed by the amalgamation of the grandeur of the sea and the divinity in our humanity. As I and my memories aged, the depths and currency of my thoughts on peace were progressively renewed.

After years of unresolved conceptual discrepancies surrounding peace, the walls of my belief system slowly crumbled under the weight of new realities of early manhood. My primitive assumptions gave way to the sobering whispers of logic, refined knowledge, and counterpoising experiences. The first of such conflicts surfaced years later, when I attempted to figure out why the number of fights and stabbings continued to mount in the serene environment of Lumley Beach. At the same time, intra-family rivalries among inhabitants continued to upset the balance of peace and stability in Waterloo. As my notion of peace evolved, I realized that neither environmental factors nor extraneous natural phenomena were comprehensively sufficient to account for the inner peace that we experienced.

That cerebral transition subsequently gave rise to my contemporary belief that peace is transactional and largely dependent on the options we exercise, particularly the choices we make in response to circumstances and events. Annexed to that assumption is the belief that our options are framed and developed based on past experiences, training, and practice, as well as our conscious assessment of prior reactions to similar situations. The pattern of choices made, together with the response offered to events and stimuli, is among the most powerful determinant of our generally perceived state of mind. The second product of this mental transition is the notion that change is unavoidable and that adapting to change is critical in the pursuit of peace.

Shaping as well as harmonizing change in an effort to attain peace is a personal and social necessity. Incontestably, one of the greatest enemies of the future is complacency or inaction in the face of change. Conversely, every step toward adapting to change and mastering the forces of change will have implications for the promotion of peace and the joy of living; for adaptability (or the ability to adjust) is the most revealing essence of human sophistication.

The Rationale for Peace

From time to time in each of our lives, events erupt, circumstances unravel, and the threat of things falling apart may translate into a reality that summons some combination of knowledge, spiritual fortitude, and character. My rationale for engaging in the examination of this phenomenon is rooted in the belief that attaining inner peace is a learned behavior that begins with the individual. It also follows that peace among people and nations can only emanate from the peace resident in individuals. As a result, changing the world begins with the individual; that is, with me!

Paradoxically, the concept of peace is one that has been copiously researched, fervently discussed, and generously explored. Though constantly sought, peace remains elusive and frequently untenable. Great scholars, thinkers, religious leaders, and commoners alike have pondered and deliberated on the nature of peace, its visible characteristics, or evidence of its existence. They have also proffered thoughtful prescriptions for its attainment. Those efforts notwithstanding, the world as we know it is rife with instances and events showing the dangerous consequences of the absence of peace. In the global context, the absence of peace is almost ubiquitous, and the repercussions can be frightening and sometimes ignominious (Nasr 2002):

> All the major religions preach peace, yet have to face occasions when war has become inevitable for one reason or the other. Christ spoke of turning the right cheek, yet for centuries in Europe major and minor wars were fought in the name of Christianity or a particular brand of Christianity. (Nasr 2002, 216)

Of course, Christians have not been the sole perpetrators of wars; neither has Christianity been the unique cause of wars. Often, as individuals, corporations, organizations, or ethnic, racial, or national groups, we have consistently failed to realize peace, and even when we infrequently do, we fall short of sustaining it. Individuals are often torn apart by the vicissitudes of life, rent by the savagery of man, and overexposed to the vibrant dynamics of nature. Without the knowledge, skills, and self-discipline to confront life's potential streams of turmoil, individuals fall prey to the demands of their physical environment of things, ideas, and knowledge, as well as to the social environment of people.

Thus, the impetus for exploring this subject is generated by the desire to sow seeds of positive change in society by jolting our consciousnesses to the limitlessness of the potential energy in peace. This endeavor is, therefore, an effort to engage and refine the trilogy of the human component (body, mind, and soul), so as to influence habit formation that will lead to the process of self-reformation and social transformation. As individuals, we are endowed with the capacity to tailor our lifestyles so we can minimize the frequency with which we succumb or surrender to turmoil, pain, malaise, and sufferings. I entertain a strong conviction that by engaging body, mind, and soul and by fully harmonizing and synchronizing them, we can summon our divine attributes, ennoble our thoughts and actions, and unlock our full potentials.

Considering the proposition, "Where ignorance is bliss, it is folly to be wise," I marry the contrarian assumption that wisdom (as reflected in acquired insight and relevant knowledge over time) should be instrumental in dismantling the baleful shroud of ignorance and pride that overshadows the attainment of peace. Certainly, there is nothing blissful about ignorance. Though ignorance may at times feign bliss, ignorance cannot be a blissful disposition. It is an orientation that is not often bereft of pernicious or deadly consequences and ramifications. As we are admonished in the Holy Scriptures (Hosea 4:6), "My people perish for lack of knowledge, because thou hast rejected knowledge, I will also reject thee." How we perceive and seek truth or falsehood, right or wrong, good or evil, sadness or joy are dependent on our acquired systems of knowledge, values, beliefs, and attitudes. Knowledge, therefore, can be empowering and is one of the legs on which peace stands.

Likewise, our notion of peace is often defined, tainted by, and predicated on what we know, believe, and value. Our sense of justice or our embrace of turmoil is shaped by how we perceive and react to people, things, and events. As an acquired disposition and not necessarily a mindless anticipation, peace is a product of our conscious reactions to the situations with which we are confronted. Thus, the often-made claim of "no justice, no peace" rebels against human nature and is of questionable validity. It is unreasonable to assume that we summon or yield to turmoil because justice is not tenable. The relationship between justice and peace is not causal. In all human societies, injustice usually coexists with peace, and peace can prevail under unjust conditions. Our reaction to injustice may or may not be peaceful. It depends on how we choose to react. An employee or servant may believe that a set of unjust demands on his/her time, talents, resources, or personhood can be provisionally accommodated. So too, a people or nation can peacefully subject themselves to policies and practices that are counterproductive to their aspirations and well-being. They may also embrace rules and conditions that are unjustly instituted or imposed on them. The actions of individuals, peoples, and nations, sometimes conceived in insensitivity, ignorance, or ineptitude, can make people or subjects peacefully espouse unjust conditions and laws. How we conceive peace or turmoil is a function of the mind. The mind or intellect, being the depot of knowledge, is therefore pivotal in experiencing, conceiving, and interpreting peace.

To live in peace often involves causing harmony from within or displacing turmoil from without. Peace is upset when a conflict from within remains unresolved. Generally, turmoil manifests itself as unresolved discrepancy. The lack of preparedness or readiness to face our chaotic world invariably becomes a recipe for inner turmoil. It is not uncommon for man's raging inner turmoil to evolve as a catalyst for conflicts with other persons with whom he interacts. Thus, it is conceivable that an increased capacity to neutralize the root causes of inner turmoil can translate into a reduction in instances of inner turmoil. It can also result in ameliorating one's ability to interact with the social and physical environment. Inner peace facilitates clarity of the inner light that enhances our capacities to interact with our world. As articulated by Lao-Tzu (Beckwith 2008, xvi), it creates the requisite condition to "use the light that dwells within you to regain your natural clarity of sight."

Closely related to the discourse on peace is the recognition of extraneous as well as innate factors that may impinge on the individual's capacity or propensity for peaceful coexistence with the external world. Innate factors couched in the accident of birth (such as the random selection dictated by genetics) or extraneous factors, such as nurture, can have consequences for how we perceive or respond to our external environment. Also, the competing claims of persons and peoples, governmental curtailment of individual freedoms, institutional regulations, or ecological or environmental conditions can equally have consequences for how we perceive and respond to our external environment.

In addition, innate factors can influence our capacity to react to stimuli in the environment. The preponderance of research evidence suggests that there is a positive correlation between an individual's ability to experience happiness and his innate psychological predisposition to peace. Certainly, the physical as well as psychological characteristics and traits with which we are born are rarely susceptible to massive change. However, through training and practice, we can dilute their counterpoising effects on our efforts to attain peace.

A close associate of the phenomenon of peace is happiness. Peace, however, transcends the limited parameters of happiness and is more permanent than a mood or state of mind that is experienced as a result of an event or some specific external stimuli. Though not synonymous, peace and happiness are interrelated, and like peace, happiness can be mediated by the individual's genetic constitution.

In his assessment of happiness, Brooks (2008, 10) noted:

> These patterns have not gone unnoticed by researchers, who have shown quite conclusively that there is a strong genetic component to happiness. Your state of mind is due in significant part to the wiring you get from your parents. Researchers concluded that at least half of one's "baseline happiness" (the fact is, the happiness

reported in the absence of unusually good or bad
life events) is hereditary.

In spite of the potential for peace to be disrupted by genetic
predisposition, the individual has ample latitude of behavioral
options or choices. These behavioral options, if adequately
mastered and appropriately applied, can promote inner peace
and peaceful interaction with our external environment. Though
our genetic makeup, circumstances, or stations in life may
influence who we are, we can take personal responsibility for
who we become. To a great extent, we humans become who we
choose to become, as is succinctly expressed in the adage, "What
we are born with is God's gift to us; what we become is our gift
to humanity." Our thoughts, words, and actions significantly
contribute to determining our states of mind as well as our stations
in life. Understanding peace, striving toward its attainment and
maintenance, and employing it as a way of life are worthy goals
that individuals and nations should seek to realize.

Competing Viewpoints on Peace

Though its meaning is usually associated with the absence
of tension within an individual or between and among persons
or nations, peace is not necessarily limited to the absence of
conflict, aggression, or war. As a likely Latin and Anglo-Norman
derivative (*pax*), *peace* generally denotes a cessation of or freedom
from disturbance, violence, or war. By extension, the word peace
suggests the "calm or tranquility" that resides in an individual,

as well as between and among individuals or groups. In this segment of the analysis, we will focus on the dual attributes of peace, first as a persistent inner state or condition and second as an experience. The concept, as analyzed in this context, focuses on peace not only as a range of human experiences but also as the culminating psycho-organic spiritual state of being that can be achieved and maintained through knowledge, contemplation, and meditation. It evolves as a lifestyle. Like any other planned and productive endeavor, peace is often seen as the product of self-discipline that results from the conscientious mastery of body, mind, and soul.

Likewise, in this analysis, peace is examined under two typologies—individual or inner peace and social peace. Individual or inner peace, in addition to being an experience, is a latent state that resides within the individual. Its external manifestation is usually in the form of human actions and demeanor that are consistently devoid of disquieting thoughts, emotions, and actions. Peace displays harmony in personal relations. In examining inner peace, one of its greatest proponents, Mahatma Gandhi, noted, "Outward peace is useless without inner peace" (Navajivan 2007, 90).

In the same vein, Desmond Tutu (Navajivan 2007, 3) asserted that when inner peace consistently assumed the embodiment of one's relationship with others, one would receive the highest accolades and esteem in the community:

> In my culture and tradition the highest praise
> that can be given to someone is *Yu, u nobuntu,*

an acknowledgement that he or she has this
wonderful quality: *ubuntu*. It is a reference to
their actions toward their fellow human beings,
it has to do with how they regard people and
how they see themselves within their intimate
relationships, their familial relationships, and
within the broader community ... the essence of
what is to be human ... they are not threatened
by the goodness in others because their own
esteem and self worth is generated by knowing
they belong to a greater whole.

Adjectives used to describe this phenomenon were hospitable,
generous, friendly, approachable, large-hearted, caring, and
compassionate. The Most Reverend Desmond Tutu affirmed
that the individuals who possessed those inner qualities and
experienced that inner state would "use their strengths on behalf
of others—the weak and the poor and the ill—and not take
advantage of anyone" (3).

Succinctly put, Tutu noted that one's knowledge of self
and others would come from the foundational premise that "I
am human because I belong." In this context, self-knowledge
is pivotal in the assessment of peace. Further, he established a
connection between the inner estimation of self and its external
manifestation in one's interaction with others—"a person is a
person through other people ... But anger, resentment, a lust for
revenge, greed, even the aggressive competitiveness that rules

so much of our contemporary world corrodes and jeopardizes our harmony" (3–4).

As a complement to individual peace, social peace (i.e., peace with others in our social environment) is often derived from inner or individual peace. On the one hand, peace usually manifests itself in the absence of tension or physical confrontation and conflicts. On the other hand, evidence of the absence of inner or individual peace is more elusive and is usually evident in the interactions of persons or people. Though this dichotomy has been established and reestablished over the years, the essential characteristics of peace, as well as the prerequisite conditions for nurturing it as a sustained measure, are still substantially misunderstood.

This two-pronged approach to looking at peace (as being a lifestyle) mirrors Plato's perspective on justice in *The Republic* (Warmington and Rouse 1956), to which he assigned two dimensions: individual and social. Thrasymachos and Socrates shared the common notion that a balanced or peaceful (intrapersonal as well as interpersonal) existence evolves from virtue and wisdom, "for frictions and hates and battles among themselves are what injustice gives them, I suppose, Thrasymachos, but justice gives friendship and a single mind; doesn't it?" (151). According to Plato, experiencing peace, as revealed in justice, is derived from the individual attaining a state of personal balance or equilibrium. The discourse on justice continued along the lines of its being a way of life: "We now come to the second question which we proposed ... The matter is no chance trifle, but how we ought to live." (152)

As the flip side or antithesis of the just man, Socrates (Warmington and Rouse 1956) evokes the image of the tyrannical man:

> The tyrannic man is ruled by the worst class of the unnecessary desires. To the lawlessness of the democratic man he adds the frenzy of lust; utterly without scruple, he is driven to boundless excess by passions he can never sate. The tyrannic man, like the tyrannic state, is slave to fear, want, every sort of misery and every sort of wickedness; he is last in happiness. (123)

The tyrannic man, according to Plato's depiction, poses two threats. The first is threat to himself. His psychological or inner state of imbalance becomes the source of his unhappiness as well as malcontent. His existence degenerates into an unhealthful lifestyle. In itself, it exudes unhappiness. On the second plane, his interaction with his external social environment (or significant others) can be generously toxic. Invariably, it originates from unhappiness, and it generates unhappiness. The spillover effect of this condition, being potently dysfunctional, may extend beyond the bounds of one's immediate social context—beyond self, family, friends, and community.

In an attempt to understand the nature of peace and the conditions that foster peace, we are to be mindful of the negative correlation between peace and turmoil. In seeking peace, we are to be deliberate in identifying strategies to facilitate its emergence and attempt to promote behavioral patterns or habits that foster the attainment of individual and social peace. The foundational assumption is that global peace can be maintained and furthered only by the concerted efforts of individuals or groups of individuals who are not only peace-loving but also peaceful.

Chapter 2

Framing Peace

> When we change the way we look at
> things, the things we look at change.
>
> —author unknown

Religious Context of Peace

Great philosophers and books of faith propagate varied
notions of peace and espouse diverse trajectories to
peace. My perspective, particularly the way I perceive and
conceive reality, is a product of my interactive experiences. The
experiences I've lived, the people with whom I have interacted,
the observations or empirical evidences I've gleaned, and
particularly the books and materials I've read are relevant. They

have all contributed to shaping my outlook on life. This chapter is a compendium of the formative literature that has profoundly influenced and shaped my perspectives on peace. In looking at the spiritual foundations of peace, Esposito (2002) notes:

> Peace is central to all three faiths. This is reflected historically in their use of similar greetings meaning "peace be upon you"; shalom Aleichem in Judaism, pax vobiscum in Christianity, and salaam alaikum in Islam. (74)

In Islam, one of the great religions of the world, peace occupies a place of significance in its teachings and practices. Muslims believe that paradise evokes peace (Qur'an 19:62), and peace is a necessary attribute of paradise (Qur'an 56:26). Semantically, "Islam means submission to peace" (Jelloun 2002, 12). Its origin suggests the word *salam*, which means "peace" and "submission to a single God, to whom we owe obedience, fidelity and loyalty."

Also, two dimensions of peace are evident in the Qur'an. The first implies social peace and is addressed in the Sharias. The Sharias furnish five pathways to social justice and peace (Ruthven 2000, 84). The second dimension focuses on inner peace. With reference to the Sufi tradition of Islam, Jelloun asserts, "Like other mystical movements in Christianity, Judaism, Hinduism and Buddhism, the Sufi path is a way to purification (tasawwuf)—a discipline of mind and body, whose goal is to directly experience the ultimate reality." Likewise, Esposito (2002,

101) affirms, "At the heart of Sufism is the belief that one's self must die, that is, one must undergo annihilation (fana) of the lower, ego-centered self in order to abide or rest (baqa) in God." Their elaborate prescriptions for attaining inner peace reside in disciplining the mind and body—letting go of all attachment to and awareness of the self and the phenomenal world.

In analyzing the spiritual journey toward inner peace in Islam, Emerick (2004, 32) identifies distinct evolutionary stages, the first of which "is activated from birth and is called the animal self. At this stage, our basic desires for food, sex, creature comforts, and wealth guide our life choices." According to Emerick, some people are permanently stuck at this stage, where they live, grow old, and die after a self-centered existence propelled by insatiable self-love and pleasure. Though alive, they are fossilized in a permanent state that is characterized by egocentrism and recurring or cyclical dysfunctional activities and events, the result of which contributes little or nothing to empowering others or improving the human condition. These persons are driven predominantly by self-love.

> No matter how rich or poor, educated or ignorant, famous or unknown, humans are susceptible to the temptations of our earthly desire for self satisfaction. Christians call such hedonists. The Qur'an often refers contemptuously to "the life of the world," describing it as nothing more than play and amusement, mutual rivalry, hoarding wealth and boasting. (31)

Within this context, peace becomes difficult to attain when individuals, groups, and even cultures limit their existence to trivial self-aggrandizing pursuits that mirror play and amusement, mutual rivalry, hoarding wealth, and boasting. Evidence abounds that persons or nations, stuck in such cycles of simplistic and banal functions, leave themselves open to the ravages of turmoil, conflicts, civil strife, or coups d'état. On a grand scale, such behavioral patterns characterize the economic and sociopolitical activities of failed nations and dysfunctional organizations and societies.

Emerick (2004, 32), citing the Islamic tradition, constructs the ultimate stage that clearly presents a prescriptive path to inner peace:

> Through a daily regimen of prayer, reflection, fasting and study, and a consciousness of morality, our heart becomes more and more at ease … when nothing in the world has a hold on us any longer. We lead lives of quiet contemplation and are not overly discomfited by any tragedy or bounty that may come our way. The third stage occurs when the soul becomes a restful self, awaiting the meeting with the Creator.

In profound ways, achieving and maintaining peace is, likewise, at the core of Buddhism. According to Chadron (2004, 26), the Buddhist priest and Tibetan meditation master notes that the absence of peace is usually the result of a hardening of the heart and our resistance to "softening what is rigid in our hearts." The nun remarks that peace does not cohabit with hatred. Based on articulated Buddhist precepts, patience is the antidote to aggression, and patience has the capacity to neutralize the mean-heartedness that often results in our harming one another.

> If these long-lived, ancient, aggressive patterns of
> mine that are the well spring only of unceasing
> woe, that lead to my own suffering as well as the
> suffering of others, if these patterns still find their
> lodging safe within my heart, how can joy and
> peace in this world ever be found? (27)

Chadron asserts that the Buddhist's journey to peace is realized through the active practice of patience that engenders the de-escalation of aggression and the cultivation of fearlessness that is both compassionate and brave.

Likewise, Hahn underscores the importance and centrality of personal peace as the first step to social peace. Hahn (2003, 6) traces a path that begins with the requisite commitment and a personal treaty to specific actions that are geared toward the cultivation and practice of peace:

> The only way out of violence and conflict is for
> us to embrace the practice of peace, to think and
> act with compassion, love, and understanding.

According to this Buddhist tradition, turmoil in individuals and among societies frequently evolves from egocentrism or overly amplified self-indulgence. The Buddhist writer cites, as a source of social turmoil, ethnocentric traditions that cause persons and nations to claim monopoly on the truth by condemning those who do not share their values and beliefs. In developing a prescription for peace, the Buddhist identified five points of "mindful" training:

- reverence for life
- generosity
- sexual responsibility
- deep listening and loving speech
- mindful compassion

Like Hahn, Das Surya (2007) traces a path to enlightenment that engenders peace and encompasses the following precepts:

- transcendental gift of generosity
- the impeccable virtue of ethical self-discipline (Do not kill; do not steal; do not deceive; do not engage in sexual misconduct; do not indulge in intoxicants.)
- the transformative practice of patient forbearance (patience in our inner and secret beings)
- the power of heroic effort
- the liberating power of mindfulness and meditation
- the universal tool of skillful means
- the profundity and vastness of spiritual aspirations
- the magic of higher accomplishments
- the perfection of awakened awareness

Das Surya believes that the Buddhist prescription, as outlined above, will lead to a "life of greater joy, clarity, peace, and wisdom than you ever thought possible."

In addition to those observations, I have sought to understand the nature of and the prerequisite conditions for peace. I have also attempted to establish a working definition that is both eclectic and comprehensive enough to withstand the exigencies of a macro-analysis of the concept. An extension of the meaning of social peace has likewise involved the conditions that prevail between or among persons, people, groups, and nations.

Cognition and Peace

Given what is known about the process of cognition, I am justified in asserting that the mind governs functions that encompass the intellectual and emotional dimensions of man. Cognition, believed to be the Latin derivative (*cogito*—"I think"), captures the totality of the human thought processes. The mind is the seat of cognitive and emotional activities. How we perceive the world is mediated upon by our intellectual state and functions (our past experiences, what we know or don't know, and how we interpret concepts and events in our environment). How and when we intervene in situations and mediate in human circumstances is largely dependent on the values imbibed and the state and content of our minds. Our notion of fear and our ease to drift into varied emotional states come from the functions of the mind in conjunction with the body. Our knowledge base, beliefs, values, and attitudes weigh heavily on how we perceive the world and how we react to stimuli from it.

Likewise, human cognition, as viewed through our thought processes, is the seed from which our actions emerge or germinate. It is conceivable that the first step toward shaping a person's attitude and behavior lies in modifying his/her thoughts. Succinctly put, I am what I think, and what I say is an outflow from the content of my thoughts. Therefore, as the cradle of our experiences, the mind houses and generates our thoughts. Usually as humans, we speak from the exuberance of our thoughts; our actions are but tangible bursts of current flowing from the confluence of the heart. In essence, our thought patterns validate our existences, define our personalities, and reveal to the world who we are. It holds true that *Cogito, ergo sum,* which may be translated as, "I think, therefore I am."

In analyzing the connection between human behavior and cognition, James Allen (2007) accentuates the power of human thought and elevates thought to the level of a reliable predictor of human behavior and determinant of human character. He appropriately summons the frequently used aphorism, "As a man thinketh in his heart so is he," in an effort to construct the link between thought and character. He likens human behavior to a plant, and the plant seed to human thoughts:

> As the plant springs from, and could not be
> without the seed so every act of a man springs
> from the hidden seeds of thought, and could
> not have appeared without them ... Act is the

blossom of thought, and joy and suffering are its
fruits; thus does a man garner in the sweet and
bitter fruitage of his own husbandry ... If one
endure in purity of thought, joy follows him as
his own shadow—sure. (3–4)

Peace is a product of character that is anchored in human thought. Deliberate human actions are almost always rooted in cognition. Our thought processes are not only the nursery of our actions, but they are also the medium through which we analyze and assess our behavioral choices. Human beings are uniquely equipped with powerful intellectual, emotional, and spiritual abilities to significantly interact with, and transform the environment. Equipped with vast cognitive capacities, humankind has the unique ability to profoundly reform the self as well as drastically transform the environment.

As a being of Power, Intelligence, and Love, and
the lord of his own thoughts, man holds the key
to every situation, and contains within himself,
that transforming and regenerative agency by
which he may make himself what he will ...
Only by much searching and mining are gold
and diamonds obtained, and man can find every
truth connected with his being if he will dig deep
into the mine of his soul. And that he is the maker
of his character, the molder of his life, and the
builder of his destiny. (Allen, 6–7)

Endowed with powerful intellectual, physical, and spiritual abilities, humankind is uniquely positioned to nurture and cultivate the body, mind, and soul, such as to dramatically alter the self and the environment. By the skillful alignment of thoughts and actions, individuals can lead a generous existence that is characterized by compassion, prosperity, and peace. Thus, the truism becomes inarguably true that, in humanity's garden of generous existence, when we cultivate enlightened thoughts, we'll reap enlightened actions. When we cultivate enlightened actions, we'll reap enlightened habits. When we cultivate habits, we'll reap a character. When we cultivate certain character traits, we'll reap a destiny. Our destinies are, therefore, sufficiently our own devices and can be directly linked to our thoughts and actions. We, as reflected in our individual lifestyles, can espouse peace and divorce turmoil. Through our thoughts and actions, we can cultivate and evoke peace; supplant or nurture ignorance; ravage the equanimity of our destinies or bequeath turmoil to posterity. As human beings, we are richly invested with the ability and power to mold our destinies by nurturing and aligning the constructive powers of body and mind with the intangible essence of the spiritual being. True to his creed, Allen (2007, 4–5) makes the following assertion:

> A noble and Godlike character is not a thing of favor or chance, but is the natural result of continued effort in right thinking, the effect of long-cherished association with Godlike thoughts. An ignoble and bestial character, by

> the same process, is the result of the continued
> harboring of groveling thoughts … in the armory
> of thought he forges the weapons by which he
> destroys himself; he also fashions the tools with
> which he builds for himself heavenly mansions of
> joy and strength and peace. By the right choice
> and true application of thought, man ascends to
> the Divine Perfection.

Thus, our thoughts are the conveyors of our actions and the harbinger of our destinies. Thoughts are invisible machinations of our destinies that transport who we are and what we will become. They become visible only when they are nakedly displayed in our actions. In our thoughts are mapped the tracks to peace or turmoil.

Spirituality and Peace

In this segment, I attempt to delve deeper into the role of the spirit or soul in our quest for peace. The soul typifies the third dimension of the human trilogy (body, mind, and soul), and it is the least tangible. It transcends both the body and mind. The function of the soul is qualified by the nature and quality of the relationship between the individual and his/her divine creator. In my analysis, the terms soul and spirit are interchangeable. Spirituality, though not synonymous with religion, may be perceived and defined in relation to one's interaction with his or her higher power or supreme being. It embodies his/her perceived divine creator. The essence of one's spirituality, as revealed in his/her relationship with divinity, may be syncretic, monotheistic, or polytheistic, real or perceived, animate or inanimate, and related or unrelated to organized religion. Peace is, therefore, the natural product of the synchronous functioning of the three components of our existence. When all three components of the trilogy are aligned and are in harmony, the individual emerges to a posture and dynamic of inner peace. By the conscious and consistent process of balancing compensation, the individual persists in restoring a dynamic state of equilibrium, which is the prerequisite condition for inner peace.

As a product of Christian values and teachings, I claim a respectable familiarity with Christian principles and doctrines. They provide a ready resource pool and dependable point of reference. Without feigning impartiality, I have drawn examples from other religious persuasions and teachings without diluting or surrendering my prominent affinity to Christian precepts.

However, my analyses proffer suggestions and make recommendations that have been gleaned from research, personal experiences, and empirical evidence. This work is an exploration that is shaped partially by my personal experiences, as I furnish readers with options to cope with life's challenges and ensure harmony with self and others in our tumultuous world. It is my hope that, like learning to sow, we will aspire toward acquiring the knowledge, skills, attitude, and practice for attaining and maintaining the requisite balance. I share Ralph Waldo Emerson's assertion, "Without a rich heart, any token of prosperity, including wealth is an ugly beggar." I ardently hope that this text will inspire the reader to aspire toward inner and social peace. As we aspire to eschew a warlike, terror-inducing existence, we will find truth in the adage, "Some die without having really lived, while others continue to live, in spite of the fact that they had died." I find consolation in acknowledging that we are both alive and hopeful! I am confident that this quest for inner and social peace will result in shaping our actions, thus enabling us to extract meaning from our temporary world, while we assign purpose to our temporal existence.

Working Definition of Peace

Our efforts at defining peace begin with the construct of inner peace. Inner peace is sometimes referred to as individual peace. This state of peace is often seen as existing in an individual who, with predictable consistency, first attains a state of psycho-organic equilibrium (horizontal balance between the mind and body). The individual, through the exercise of self-discipline and contemplation, gains mastery in attaining and maintaining a stable and balanced vertical relationship with his/her divine creator. Achieving, sustaining, and restoring peace often appears to be the result of processes that are physical (of the body), cognitive and affective (of the mind), and spiritual (of one's relationship with his/her supreme being). It is believed to involve the delicate balance between and among the body, mind, and soul of an individual. Psychologists and social scientists frequently advance the claim that critical, unresolved intrapersonal conflicts are the usual causes and theater of turmoil.

Social peace, on the other hand, often reveals itself as the product of balancing an individual's needs, aspirations, and motivations with those of persons or people in his or her social environment. It may thus be construed as an extension and manifestation of individual peace within the context of the varied demands of the people with whom we interact. Developing a repertoire of options that lead to restoring peace in response to the challenges of others is a major motivation for my endeavor.

Examples are aplenty in our personal lives, in which conflict or turmoil is averted by the manner in which we react to other human beings and situations in life. Our reaction may reflect the biblical tenets as recorded in the Holy Bible: "A soft answer turneth away wrath, but a harsh word stirs up anger" (Proverbs 15:1). On the other hand, scores of human lives have been lost to tumultuous events such as street riots, gang squabbles, and road rage, most of which are avoidable. In varying degrees of involvement, some of us have unnecessarily engaged in violent conflicts at home, at work, or during recreation, resulting in substantial interpersonal conflicts and even greater organizational disruption. Whether we are looking at our individual responses in our interaction with others or looking at international relations among nations, peace and turmoil usually ensue from our actions, in response to the challenges imposed by events, individuals, or groups.

Too frequently, we allow others (often people with transient influence on our lives) to steal our peace. Self-knowledge plays an important role in how we perceive ourselves in the face of the comments and actions of others. It also determines how easily we surrender our tranquility and peace when faced with pressures from without.

Attaining peace, therefore, involves maintaining balance between and among the three dimensions of our human existence. Through the eyes of Brenner (2003), the Hebrew word *shalom* is a semantic approximation of the word *peace*. It denotes the presence of unity or balance, but it also evokes the Hebrew derivative of *shalam*, which is associated with "making restitution" and "restoring wholeness or completeness." It is claimed that it was within this context that David, in the book of Psalms (Psalm 122:6), admonished believers to pray for the peace of Jerusalem. According to Brenner, "The common phrase shalu shalom yerushalayim is beyond the idea of peace."

This discourse subscribes to a notion of peace that is eclectic and transcends the delimiting pedantic interpretation of the concept. Peace, in this discourse, is not just the condition or state of sustained personal equilibrium. It is a way of life that is dictated by a union between the human and the spiritual dimensions of individuals that results in seamless equanimity and tranquility. It is a deliberate lifestyle that is achieved through repeated acts of contemplation, self-equilibration and practice. In the Old Testament of the Holy Bible, peace is considered a divine gift that is the product of righteousness and a direct antithesis of wickedness. In the New Testament, however, peace is viewed as a direct consequence of obedience to God's rules and commandments, where spiritual peace bears a direct, positive correlation with perpetual peace of mind. Happiness and joy are the resultant profits (Achtemeier 1985, 766). Peace is, therefore, a product of godliness and righteousness. In the New Testament, we see a more expansive notion of peace: "Peace I leave with you, my peace I give to you, not as the world giveth, give I unto you. Let not your heart be troubled, nor let it be afraid" (John 14:27).

In this narrative, as in the context mentioned above, the definition of peace establishes a distinction between the peace of this world and divinely inspired peace (i.e., peace derived from the Word). It contrasts with the peace of this world, and the experience is devoid of anxiety or fear. It is a way of life that can be emulated and replicated; it involves all the dimensions of human existence. This definition, of necessity, underscores the centrality of the third dimension of human existence—the spiritual or ethereal. It is experienced not only in this world but also outside or beyond this world and in conjunction with the divine.

Thus, though peace may be observed through the lenses of inner peace and social peace, the concept conjointly manifests itself on three planes: body, mind, and soul. The body, which is the most visible component of humankind, is but a physical and physiological edifice that is conspicuously degradable. It serves primarily as the temporal and temporary encasement of psychological and physiological (biological) organs and systems. Satisfying the biological needs and harmonizing the physical as well as physiological functions of our beings are of equivalent importance in our quest for a balanced or peaceful life. What we ingest; when and how we eat; what we touch, feel, see, inhale, and exhale; and the conditions under which we nurture our physical existence are all crucial in our efforts to maintain peace.

Our efforts at identifying sensations, perceiving experiences, and assigning meaning to objects and events are initiated at this level. The physical body is not only the repository of human experiences but also the gateway to human feelings and sensations. How we use, treat, and maintain our physical bodies matters! That's the nursery of personal peace.

The mind resides in the body and is a function of the body. Its functions are tied to those of the body. The mind, being the seat of intellectual and emotional activities, governs our thoughts and emotions. Developing the mind is a critical attribute of peace. Likewise, a troubled mind is a recipe for turmoil, and a mind that is not in union with either the spiritual or the corporal cannot achieve equilibrium. Invariably, an unbalanced, underdeveloped, or underutilized mind is both a consequence and forerunner of disquietude.

The third dimension of peace is defined by our relationship with our Supreme Being or creator. This relationship is vividly established in Hebrews 12:14–18.

> Make every effort to live in peace with everyone and to be holy; without holiness no one will see the LORD. See to it that no one falls short of the grace of God and that no bitter root grows up to cause trouble and defile many. See that no one is sexually immoral, or is godless like Esau, who for a single meal sold his inheritance rights as the oldest son. Afterward, as you know, when he wanted to inherit this blessing, he was

rejected. Even though he sought the blessing with tears, he could not change what he had done. You have not come to a mountain that can be touched and that is burning with fire; to darkness, gloom and storm;

Within this framework, seeking to live in harmony with others is recommended. Thus, peace is a way of life that is the ultimate product of righteous living, as prescribed by the Word. A righteous lifestyle can only be achieved through connection with the spiritual realm. Thus, the spiritual dimension of our existence provides access to the Supreme Being and generates the blueprint for a peaceful lifestyle. Righteousness is, therefore, an indispensable component of peace, for peace cannot be achieved without righteousness. It reflects the harmonious functioning that results from a healthy balance within, between, and among the body, mind, and soul.

Chapter 3

Manifestations of Turmoil

> To the primitive mind, salient proposals
> for change languish, while the trivial
> excels in importance, thus underscoring
> the reality that the true measure of
> sophistication is adaptability.

Dimensions of Turmoil

The fact that I am human is incontestable. Equally incontestable is the claim that I am gregarious, because I am human. My fate and my peace could be directly or indirectly tied to the actions and machinations of the other occupants of this global village. My individual peace would, therefore, be greatly compromised (if not threatened) by myriad circumstances and events, over which I could exercise little or no control. Knowledge about my environment or the world is a necessary resource in the search for peace. The need for knowing the world and being adequately informed and equipped to avoid pitfalls is of critical importance.

The ever-changing dynamics of our contemporary environment, coupled with our inability to respond promptly or adequately to changes in our society, renders peace elusive and tenuous. In an uncertain and constantly changing world, where we transact business and interact with others with much greater frequency, complexity, and volume, maintaining peace becomes a predictable uncertainty. It also becomes a potential casualty in the complex mix of personal relationships, business, politics, and trade. These changes in society make it feasible to share and employ people and their material resources at breathtaking speeds and with almost effortless ease across the borderless universe of the electronic media.

Billions of dollars flow into, between, and among individual interests, business organizations, and central banks with the click of a button. Persons and groups can initiate conflicts, recruit warriors, or engage in a battle without leaving their homes or towns or without ever crossing geographic borders. Wealth can be amassed overnight as rapidly as fortunes evaporate, while the lives of so many are alarmingly overtaken by anxiety and turmoil. The speed with which we do business, the complexity of the business environment, and the technological sophistication of the modes of transaction constitute a potential source of conflict and turmoil for the unsuspecting and seasoned participant alike.

Likewise, cyber technology bears great capacity to facilitate and forge distant personal and international relationships. It allows for material or emotional investments to be exploited, used, or abused by sometimes unknown and unauthorized parties. It also allows for love triangles as well as terror cells to be deceptively constructed or deconstructed across continents. Webs of deadly plots of mass destruction can be woven, and business transactions can be consummated thousands of miles away from distant sources. With unbelievable ease, national governments and political processes can be undermined, corrupted, or rendered ineffective and chaotic by unknown parties, foreign saboteurs, or counterfeit interests. Inhumane, deceptive, and faceless criminal acts can be perpetrated across nations and oceans in the blink of an eye. Scam artists from distant internet cafés can sneak into fortified domiciles and business ventures with incalculable ease and reckless abandon. Victims as well as perpetrators of these actions invariably have to contend with the grim consequences of some of these transactions. Contemporary lifestyles have generated as many opportunities as challenges, and persons who are least prepared to deal with these challenges are the most susceptible to anguish and turmoil.

Often, in some of these societies, the practice of unrestrained liberalism seems to thrive, and morality becomes as relative as irrelevant. In some other societies, including ours, the distinction between freedom and frivolity is constantly eroded and blurred. Routine human activities are rendered scary and unpredictable. As the creative genius in humankind continues to excel, our capacity for self-restraint shows no sign of keeping pace with the novel demands on society. In a global village where the moral fabric of its constituent societies progressively degenerates and where an inadequate (if not nonexistent) common code of ethics or morality prevails, the output from creative and powerful technology may constitute a well-disguised Pandora's box.

Also, the potential to upset peace is greatly elevated as a result of the scope, speed, and nature of human interactions in a constantly shrinking global village. The fast-paced changes in technology have broadened our sphere of influence, widened our theater of operations, and consequently obliged us to assume expanded duties and responsibilities while exposing us to potential rifts, conflicts, and turmoil. The added responsibilities associated with these expanded opportunities pose tremendous challenges to individuals and societies alike. The uncertainty and unpredictability resulting from our great technological strides have far-reaching implications for inner peace and turmoil.

A person's inner turmoil, like extreme ignorance, may at times assume an orientation that is latent but potentially dangerous. It raises its head in our actions and often may be couched in a sustained state of disequilibrium within and among the human trilogy of body, mind, and soul. Such life-changing events impose strains or stress on the human trilogy. The strains and stresses then become an incubator for turmoil, as more turmoil invariably exudes more stress. The dangers associated with stress or turmoil mirror Goewey's (2014, 6) assertion:

> The seminal research on human performance
> by Wesley Sime at the University of Nebraska

concluded that ... "the greater the likelihood that you'll make bad decisions." Communication will tank, aggression and escape behaviours will swamp your ability to work collaboratively, and the intolerance for ambiguity that stress produces will derail your capacity for creative problem solving.

Though, in many ways, technology has increased the ease and precision with which certain functions are executed, it has also enormously disrupted certain routines in our personal and corporate lives. While reducing the amount of time and effort needed to perform a variety of tasks (such as computation, clerical or household chores, the production of goods, or the performance of certain monotonous and repetitive functions), technology has produced a plethora of high-tech tools and gadgets. These tools and gadgets usurp our time, squander our leisure, and jeopardize the attainment of peace. Some of us seize every opportunity to talk on the phone, text, and surf the internet, even in the most inappropriate and dangerous of circumstances. A major source of turmoil in contemporary human society is the technology-induced demands and impositions on our time, attention, talents, and resources. The machine (like our cellular phones, tablets, and drones) is becoming the master. We are quick to answer its calls, dance to its tunes, and precipitously obey its commands. It is not just a tool. At times, it is elevated to an object of trepidation, imposing its arguably unearned authority on its user. Often, it directs the affairs of the human being, and humankind has become subordinate and subservient to it. In the absence of an adopted code of morality, society, including the quality of life, degenerates; for technology without a faithful moral compass is fatefully akin to a ship without a rudder. Our inner peace is often displaced by the resultant disquietude generated by our technological know-how. With disturbing frequency, the trilogy of body, mind, and soul is upset, as our peace is invariably reduced to a casualty of our own technological advancement.

In equally striking ways, our physical and physiological well-being is directly linked to the type of food we eat (organic or genetically altered, processed or unprocessed, and so on), the type of air we breathe (clean or pollutant-laden), and the type of physical world with which we interact (devoid of or rife with noise, asbestos, plastic, nonbiodegradable contaminants, chemicals, carcinogens, etc.). Our capacity for peace is profoundly compromised when technology is neither appropriately used nor responsibly managed. In a number of ways, the inappropriate use of technology continues to pose threats to humanity and human civilization. In like manner, powerful and dangerous instruments of mass destruction can be easily concealed (because of their size or technological sophistication), transported, and detonated from locations far and wide, with devastating precision and potency. Our notion of safety and security is thus greatly disrupted and altered by the destruction that some of these devices can cause.

Conversely, we accrue great benefit from the appropriate use of technology. Therefore, though employing modern-day technology may yield great turmoil, in essence, technology is a neutral force. When appropriately used, the tangible and intangible component of technology has enabled humankind to significantly improve his/her standard of living and quality of life. The neutrality of technology is shattered only when humankind puts technology into use. Therefore, it matters how we humans choose to use technology. The social pressures to use technology, the type of technology we choose, the varied technological concepts and devices we put into use, and the consequences of using technology influence our states of mind, with powerful implications for our capacity to experience peace or turmoil.

Human Anguish and Turmoil

Since the earliest of human civilizations, humans have always sought to master their environment and control their destiny. Controlling our destinies has involved the invention and use of agricultural tools and equipment. Without ceasing, however, humans continue to refine their use of weapons of war. As individuals, groups, or nations, we have devoted a great proportion of our time, effort, and material resources to alimenting our inclination for war at the expense of mastering the attainment of peace.

Among the first-known human inventions were agricultural tools, instruments of war, and weapons intended to maim, kill, or destroy others in efforts to ensure dominance and bring opposing forces to their knees. With similar consequences, the insatiable desire to own or control the world's limited resources has plunged human societies into a constant state of friction and antagonism. In an effort to attain or maintain coveted positions of dominance, societies have inhumanely resorted to excesses in individualism, nepotism, sexism, ethnocentrism, racism, and nationalism. An incalculable amount of resources has been devoted to bellicose intentions aimed at acquiring weapons of mass destruction. Nations have hastened to acquire nuclear weapons, join the arms race, and invest huge sums of money in instruments of war. Throughout the ages, humans have (advertently or inadvertently) been actively engaged in pugnacious intentions and petulant actions. A good number of our concerted actions have contributed to fomenting war and turmoil, as we subvert and abort peace. The prospects for mass destruction and the threat of war, terrorism, and the annihilation of humanity undermine our individual and corporate feelings and notions of peace. It is not surprising that among persons, ethnic groups, and nations, advocacy for peace continues with unabated crescendo.

Just as nations strive for political, socio-cultural, and economic hegemony, individuals—knowingly or unknowingly, deliberately or inadvertently—also become committed participants in the imagined race to the top. Some label it the rat race. Others call it "life in the fast lane." Getting to the fast lane, however, and staying in the fast lane requires lots of energy, savoir faire, and the goodwill of others or some wile with providence. Competition with others invariably involves being ranked among others, based on standards that are defined and applied by others. Achieving some semblance of success and displaying the various status symbols for society's consumption and approbation are often the source of rivalry and great misery. They are also the usual impetus for an endless search for social commendation and approval.

In addition to the mindless craving for tokens of social status and materialistic prosperity, far too many members of society persistently engage in seeking the various trappings enshrined in symbols of socioeconomic mobility. For want of these status symbols, we sometimes dive into unfathomable depths of self-destructive behavior, despair, frustration, and even acts of brazen mendacity. In the chaos occasioned by our mindless cravings for social recognition and tokens of materialistic prosperity, inner peace is often submerged into oblivion.

In addition, the unrestrained and sometimes impassioned quest for social approval and approbation often leads the undisciplined mind to indulge in acts of acute individualism and self-centeredness—acts that often reflect an affinity for some of the most disabling and dysfunctional vices of society. Extreme self-centeredness, usually concealed in arrogance, is almost always a nursery for what I consider the six most destructive sources of turmoil: greed, deceit, anxiety, anger, envy, and hate.

With rare exceptions, human disquietude is a product of one or some combination of the vices or character failures associated with hate, arrogance, deceit, and anxiety caused by impatience, greed, or envy (HADAGE). From the least significant to the most global and acute of human sufferings, the roots of human turmoil are often deeply buried in one of these vices. Our insensitivity to the needs of our fellow human beings; disrespect for the comfort and convenience of others; barbaric acts of terrorism; dysfunctional national, racial, or ethnic sentiments; or our persistent desire to overshadow others or steal the limelight at the expense of the dignity of others usually comes as a result of selfishness or greed.

Our quest for political dominance and political pilfering are not unusually generated by our desire to control power, space, or wealth. In like manner, interpersonal conflicts, intra-family disputes, neighborhood and turf wars, common acts of road rage, playing excessively loud music in public or disturbing the peace, and other ills of society often stem from a desire to dominate or monopolize space, the air waves, or other societal resources. On a global scale, wars, coups d'état, the rigging of political elections, deliberate abuse of political power, cheating and lying, and coveting the material or human resources of others are emblematic of character failures that emanate from one or more of these vices. Generally, inner peace and social peace are threatened when any of those character traits assumes dominance in human interactions.

Needs/Wants Satisfaction

An important consideration in the equation of inner peace and turmoil is the prominence of needs and wants. Needs and wants are often the primary motivation of human behavior. Human behavior almost always is dictated by the desire to satisfy needs and reduce wants. People's insatiable desire to satisfy their needs and unlimited wants, in spite of the limited availability of resources, is a common cause of conflicts and source of turmoil. Individuals, organizations, and nations engage in bloody acts of violence in efforts to claim or acquire wealth. Wars are fought over territories, and territories have been lost in struggles to control wealth. Innumerable lives have been lost in the constant quest for material wealth.

In some societies, generating profit is at the core of almost every human transaction. In other less-affluent societies, where governmental regulations are more casual, profiteering is the usual order (if not the very engine) of business. Thus, in seeking to satisfy their needs and wants, some often end up generating grandiose future wants for themselves, as they reduce the chances of others to satisfy their own basic needs. Since the primary motivation of human behavior is the satisfaction or reduction of needs, our states of mind, our behavioral options, and our lifestyles are all influenced by how we seek to address our wants and satisfy our needs.

Consistent with Maslow's theory (Maslow 1968), human needs are universal and hierarchical, and even the satisfaction of the most basic of these needs is temporary. According to Maslow's Hierarchy of Needs, human conduct is primarily shaped by a person's disposition to satisfy needs, which may be physical or physiological, psychological, sociological, or reflective of self-actualization and that transcend cultural or geographic boundaries.

In addition, the information explosion, the ready accessibility of individuals and organizations to persons and businesses, and the speed with which we acquire information and data have implications for how we opt to address our needs and determine our wants. The information explosion has likewise resulted in the introduction of new technologies with their accompanying demands. Understanding these technologies, acquiring and utilizing them, and coping with their demands constitute a powerful source of tension and turmoil.

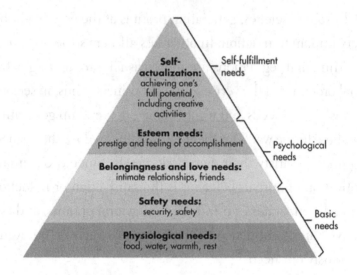

Maslow's Hierarchy of Needs, Figure 3-1
Adopted from McLeod, S. A. (2014). Maslow's
Hierarchy of Needs.

Our constant struggle to satisfy our needs and address our wants tracks our journeys and paths toward peace. Our need for food, shelter, and clothing is the most elementary of needs. So too are our notions of and desires to satisfy safety needs. Individuals and nations may react to acts of terrorism differently, based on their perception of how safe or secure they want to be in and out of their communities. Their military or economic might, the possible consequences of retaliation, or the level of deterrence they intend to impose or tolerate can also factor in the choices they make. Likewise, the relative permanence of our episodes of physiological-need sensation, coupled with the virtual limitlessness of our individual wants is a key determinant of how we perceive our world and how we react to persons, events, and situations. In the same way, our desire to love and be loved and our chosen path to self-actualization and the externalization of self-esteem are all crucial in shaping our actions, habits, destiny, and—above all—our inner peace.

Personally, biblical principles and tenets have consistently steered my response to needs and wants. Under the tutelage and guidance of my parents, Lily and Edward P. Nicol, and guided by biblical teachings, I imbibed a healthy sense of responsibility toward responding to and adequately satisfying physical and physiological needs. These teachings provide a framework for targeting hard work and creativity as measures to address my personal physical needs, while exercising moderation and principled modesty in evaluating my wants and consumptions.

As a young boy nearing the age of ten, I was stunned by my father's unmistakable disapproval of my anger toward one of my older brothers, who had stealthily gone through my personal belongings and taken my favorite pair of socks for his evening escapade. With unrestrained anger and unforgiving rants, I made a beeline to my father's home office to lodge a complaint and expose what I perceived as my brother's irresponsible action. I should have known better. My father responded to my outburst with tamed disapprobation. In what seemed to be an endless test of endurance and intestinal fortitude, I listened to his scornful silence. The quiet storm later followed. After subsequently having suffered the sting of six strokes of the cane and the pangs of an uneasy conscience, I learned from him the valuable lesson that my attempting to humiliate my older brother was not an act of love, and that sharing with others, particularly a brother in need, is the true mark of Christian love.

During my infant nurture, I learned to appreciate the need to develop the capacity to satisfy my biological needs and adequately assess and respond to my safety needs, while maintaining healthy human relationships that are founded on love and trust. At an early age, I inculcated the foundational Christian principle that all relationships—vertical (divine) as well as horizontal (human and physical)—are to be founded on the Christian centerpiece of love (Matthew 22:34–40; John 3:16). Loving God and loving man, the two foundational pillars of Christianity, define the orientation of my moral compass. My needs for self-esteem are tempered with humility, while my need for self-actualization is qualified by an inner drive to nurture humanity and improve the human condition. My desire to enter the teaching profession, touch and uplift lives, and ultimately improve the human condition was derived from my parents' precepts and examples. Their love and knowledge of God, their adherence to Christian principles, and their commitment to transmit Christian values to my siblings and me, pure and unsullied, were at the crux of their parenting obligations and endeavors.

The kind care and attention of my parents—Lily, a philanthropist and prayer-warrior, and Edward, a renowned educator and church worker—furnished me with the tools for a purpose-driven existence that was nurtured in a childhood environment replete with precepts and practices of virtue. Imbibing these precepts, I began to conceive of the boundless possibilities of love. The knowledge of a higher power, the unflinching faith in God and His Son, Jesus, and His all-consuming love (John 3:16) and grace proved to be the unavoidable but most dependable rudder in my life. I realized that my being a lower power, made in His image and likeness, I shared in His divinity in spite of my frail humanity. Therefore, as a living creature in the image and likeness of God (Genesis 1:26–28), I am charged with cultivating and transmitting the seeds of goodness implanted in me, as a measure to obey God's will and enrich posterity. Throughout my teenage years, I developed a deep appreciation for an outlook on life that would strengthen the body, fortify the mind, and uplift the spirit (1 Corinthians 6:19–20).

Throughout my infant and adolescent Christian nurture, I came to marry the belief that each of our lives on earth is defined by the depth and quality of the human relationships each of us nurtures. At the core of our existence is the question: "How passionate are we about touching the lives of others, and how instrumental are we in improving the lot of others?" (1 Peter 3:8). Also, my experiences oriented me toward the belief that as long as we continue to measure human progress in quantitative terms that are based on what and how much we can accumulate (as opposed to how well we can relate to each other's needs and aspirations), conflicts and turmoil will abound, and they will dictate the course of human relations. When the cycle of unmet needs, acute material wants, and despair is allowed to fester, then we limit our temporal mission to sowing seeds of turmoil. In themselves, the unmet human needs are stressors. The inability to promptly and adequately address these needs constitutes a catalyst for mental, physical, spiritual, political, economic, or social pressures that, when ignored, can emerge as an invitation to turmoil. Usually among humans, turmoil is generated by stressors that are left unresolved. The effects of poorly managed stressors manifest themselves as stress, which is the primary origin of turmoil.

Stress and Inner Peace

Among the most destabilizing forces that negate the attainment and maintenance of inner peace is stress. In an excerpt from the American Psychological Association's *Annual Survey on Stress in America*, Goewey (2014, 1) noted that the data from the survey "portrays a picture of high stress and ineffective coping mechanisms that appear to be ingrained in our culture, perpetuating unhealthy lifestyles and behaviors for future generations."

By the same token, Charlesworth and Nathan (2004) remarked that in addition to diminishing the quality of life, stress affects the way we think, feel, and relate to one another. It can also result in the premature death of its victim. The authors remarked,

> The effects of long-term stress on our mental health can be devastating ... Occasionally, we may feel tense and explosive. Sometimes we find ourselves compulsively repeating meaningless tasks in an attempt to control our lives. At times, we act impulsively without thinking about

the consequences. At other times, we have
exaggerated fears of such simple acts as leaving
our house, travelling by airplane, or riding in
an elevator.
(14–15)

According to Charlesworth and Nathan (2004), as instances of
stress increase, the material cost associated with stress continues to
mount. They noted the following wastage in financial resources:

- $300 billion is lost annually by American industry from
  stress-related reasons, such as lost time, extra cost of
  health insurance, replacing employees
- $246 billion is lost annually by American industry from
  substance abuse
- $200 billion is spent annually by Americans for treatment
  and lost productivity
- $100 billion is lost annually in health care by American
  businesses as a result of chronic pain
- $32 million workdays a year are lost in stress-related
  absenteeism and lost productivity

In terms of the human toll, the statistics culled from the
authors are sobering. Added to the billions of dollars spent each
year, millions of lives are lost to the ravages of stress-related
disorders. Correctional facilities are overcrowded with persons
who are incarcerated as a result of stress-related conduct and
other mental health disorders. The authors indicated that human
sufferings and casualty associated with stress could be incalculable

and priceless. The following tabular presentation of the relevant statistics exposes the enormity of stress-related disorders.

Number of Americans plagued with stress-related disorders, Figure 3-2

Number of American Victims per Year	Type of Stress-Related Disorder
67 million	Suffer from major heart disease or blood vessel disease
69 million	Suffer from high blood pressure
18 million	Suffer from alcoholism
31 million	Suffer from diabetes associated with obesity and physical inactivity
108 million	Adults who are obese or overweight
300,000	Suffer preventable death annually as a result of modifiable behavioral patterns

American Stress-Related Drug Use, Figure 3-3

Doses or People per Year	Drug-Related Activity
6 billion doses	Tranquilizer prescriptions each year
4 billion doses	Muscle-relaxant prescriptions
4 billion doses	Antidepressant prescriptions
5 billion doses	Pain-killer prescriptions
4 million people	Prescription drug abuse (pain relievers, stimulants, sedatives, or tranquilizers)

Almost every adult knows something about stress but few are familiar with the dangerous effects of stress and the various ways stress manifests itself. Also, few may be familiar with the causes of stress. One is, therefore, tempted to ask, "What is stress?" Simply put, the challenges with which we are confronted in life are called stressors. Individuals react or respond differently to different stressful situations or stressors. Stress is the effect of the individual's reaction to a stressful situation or stressor. The effect of a given stressor may vary from one individual to the other. For example, on hearing a gunshot in close proximity and without notice, each of two visiting tourists would react differently. It may cause stress to one but not to the other. It is also likely that the stress or stress level that is generated by the gunshot would vary widely between the two tourists, based on a variety of factors.

Notwithstanding the variance in our individual responses to stressors, Charlesworth and Nathan (2004) claimed that among all of the previously identified stressors, work-related stressors would be considered the most prevalent and direst of stress-related consequences in the United States. The following findings from the survey indicate how some of the stressors rank:

- One-fourth of employees rank their job as the most disturbing or dominant stressor.
- Three-fourths of employees believe that they nowadays have more job-related stressors to contend with than their counterparts did a generation ago.
- Work-related stress responses originate more from health-related issues than any other factors.

They further identified two types of stress responses: short term (which is often characterized by physical, emotional, or behavioral warning signs, such as sweating, stomach jittering, dry mouth) and long term (which may be characterized by poor job performance, reduced sex drive, overeating, or depression). Though both short-term and long-term stress responses have negative effects on the individual, the effects of long-term stress responses are more durable and much more pernicious. Here are fifteen major classifications of stressors:

o   emotional (fears, anxieties, worries, etc.)

o   work (work-related tensions and pressures, asking for a raise, meeting work deadlines, etc.)

o   chemical (drugs, alcohol use or abuse, food or water contaminants, caffeine, etc.)

o   physical (weight gain or weight loss, sleep, nutrition, diet, pregnancy, etc.)

o   family (the birth of a child, family structure or marriage-related, child care or child safety)

o   social (interactions with the individual or with groups, attending conferences, parties, etc.)

o   decision (making difficult choices in life; financial or occupational decisions)

o   phobic (exaggerated fears of objects, events, places, animals, or situations)

o   disease (long- or short-term chronic disorders, congenital health-related disorders, such as diabetes or high blood pressure)

o   pain (aches and pains of injuries and diseases; pain that is triggered by stress)

o   media (printed news, TV or radio broadcast, movies, etc.)

o   terrorism (distant violent acts of terrorism, heightened airport/shopping malls/public gathering awareness)

o   environmental (noise, smoke, extreme heat or cold, glare of the sun)

o   change (adjusting to change, any alteration to routine, coping with life's changes)

o   commuting (traffic jams, road or rail accidents, speeding motorists, tardiness, etc.)

In humans, stressors are countless, and they lurk around every corner of our interaction with our inner or outer world. Also, stressors are inescapable, and as long as we ply the routes of our temporal existence, we are sure to encounter stressors. However, though stressors are inevitable, stress is evitable. Every perceived situation in life is a potential source of stress. Though every episode of stress stems from one or more stressors, not all stressors result in stress. The nature of the reaction or response offered to one or more stressors determines whether we experience stress or not. Thus, stress is of our own making. It is a creation that is borne in our response to one or more challenges in life. By our conduct, we can create, neutralize, or aggravate stress, depending on how we choose to respond to the various stimuli and challenges that confront us.

In concluding, I underscore the foundational premise that life affords us an endless stream of challenges or stressors. Our needs and wants constitute the most potent and persistent summonses to action. The necessity of satisfying our needs is further complicated by the demands imposed by our desire to acquire, use, and attain familiarity with technology. How we respond to the various challenges confronting us will determine our ability to create or neutralize stress, with stress being one of the most elementary manifestations of turmoil.

Chapter 4

Owning and Sowing
the Joy of Peace

The use to which any material or human resource is put is a testament to the character and intentions of the agents managing change.

Pathways to Peace

Far from claiming perfection or feigning omniscience, I acknowledge the potential fallacy inherent in any suggestion that my work is prescriptive. It is not. Rather, my endeavor is to share my personal experiences, coping strategies, precepts, and practices that have been instrumental in minimizing turmoil. Personally, I have embraced certain precepts and practices in an effort to give direction to my life. Putting these precepts and practices into use has involved the making of choices. The outcome of these choices has shaped my interaction with my God, my family and friends, and my total external environment of people, ideas, and things. I hope that by reading of my life experiences, the reader will be empowered and enabled. I envisage that the reader will establish a point of reference through which (s)he may find elements of similarity or congruence that are worthy of further investigation, replication, or emulation. It is also conceivable that, for others, it may provoke deliberate acts of introspection and profound events of retrospection, with a view to developing strategies for neutralizing turmoil and accentuating inner peace.

I, therefore, find comfort in the hope that as an enabling exercise, my efforts at sowing seeds of peace will mimic the work of a planter of seeds, as opposed to that of a traveler embarking on a journey. There is a distinction: embarking on a journey may primarily entail being transported from one location to another, but sowing seeds requires the effort, skills, and assiduity of the sower. Sowing seeds underscores the centrality of commitment and deliberate efforts that bring about the desired outcome. Thus, sowing seeds of peace entails the acquisition and application of the requisite orientation, knowledge, and skills to make appropriate choices in life that will bring about inner peace.

My Path toward Peace

My pursuit of peace has been shaped by the evolution of my experiences and thoughts, as well as by the cultivation of a repertoire of behavioral options over time. Bear in mind that no two persons experience the same set of events and stimuli or react to identical situations in the same way. I pay due respect to individual differences and acknowledge that we human beings are more alike than we are different. Therefore, we can apply successful approaches to solving problems as well as implement workable solutions to identical or similar problems.

Through introspective retrospection, I have traced my personal pathway toward peace on the foundation of the following three sets of pillars (the three sixes):

- six foundational principles guiding my thoughts and conduct
- six life-changing events and defining moments depicting personal challenges and bouts with turmoil
- six self-directed maintenance activities to cultivate and maintain a culture of inner peace

Generally, principles are foundational truths on which our core belief systems are anchored. Our beliefs inform and govern our personal behavior. Similar to sowing seeds, the six basic principles I have identified create the conditions that foster germination and nurturing. These conditions (without which germination is grossly impeded or fatally compromised) provide one of the three legs that support my quest for peace. These principles provide a disciplined procedure for ensuring a rich and empowering environment, where seeds of peace can germinate and blossom. They are the foundation of my quest for peace. The guiding principles guide my thoughts and actions, and they provide the basis for my conscious responses to situations.

The six life-changing events or defining moments reflect the events that have profoundly (if not irreversibly) shaped and tested my character. As formative agents of character, the life-changing events yield experiences and opportunities that build character. They also generate challenges that necessitate serious contemplation. Personally, these events have jolted my consciousness and presented opportunities for profound thoughts and actions that would test and shape character. They constitute the second set of legs that support my quest for peace. These life-changing events were necessary occurrences; if not appropriately managed, they would have had the potential to jeopardize or overwhelm the prosperity and survival of the seeds of change. These uncommon life experiences deeply impacted all levels of my human triad. They have toughened my body, stretched my mind, and strengthened my soul. Like cultivating the soil, my reacting constructively to life-changing events has led to a qualitative change in my outlook on life. Also, experiencing those life-changing events has resulted in significant personal growth and character building. The events often engendered significant changes in my lifestyle. In addition, they resulted in actions and routine activities that, like tilling the soil and cultivating seeds of peace, required contemplation and conscientious change in routine activities, as well as in my character.

These life-changing events may vary from one individual to another in number and intensity, but those that I experienced could be characterized by the following:

- The events were sudden, often unplanned, and overwhelmingly presented uncommon challenges.
- They involved a change of environment or significant alteration in my environment.
- They required the intervention or use of additional resources (human, physical, pecuniary, etc.).
- They required action based on hope, and they summoned my faith in God.
- They resulted in the justification for great optimism involving greater challenges.
- They exposed the need for deep analysis, meditation, and contemplation on the issues caused by the challenges.

The six self-directed maintenance activities provide the third of three legs that support my quest for peace. They involve providing the tools and resources that aid my efforts at cultivating and maintaining a culture of peace. They are maintenance activities that nourish the body, enrich the mind, or fortify the soul. These maintenance activities ensure a continued and refreshed capacity for a peaceful existence that is characterized by self-renewal and self-defined prosperity.

In retrospect, the following are the three sixes, representing (1) the six guiding principles, (2) the six life-changing events, and (3) the six maintenance activities that have furnished the tripod on which my quest for peace has evolved. These principles have shaped my thoughts and, to a great extent, dictated my general deportment.

Six Guiding Principles and Practices in Making My Personal Choices in Life

- ❖ Put God first, and surrender all to Him.
- ❖ Selflessly show love for God and humankind in all undertakings, with a view to treating others as you want them to treat you.
- ❖ Ceaselessly and diligently, seek to know the *world* and understand the *Word*.
- ❖ Translate knowledge of God and of the world into purpose and actions for daily living.
- ❖ Show due respect for God, humankind, and all of God's creation, but fear no one.
- ❖ Subdue improper and irregular passions, and compete with none but self.

Principles, Guiding Thoughts, Words, and Actions toward Peace

- • Put God first, and surrender all to God.

In every significant undertaking, I have learned to put God first and, when my human faculties are exhausted, to surrender all to Him. Also, I give thanks and show appreciation to God, even under the worst of circumstances. In everything, I give thanks and praise to my God. When I am about to lose hope and think I have reached the end of my endurance, I surrender all to God, with bended knees and prayerful heart. By putting God first, I allow my steps to be ordered by a supreme power who is greater than me. He is my God. From experience, I know that when God leads and I follow, I can never go wrong or drift astray. I draw strength from the words found in Psalm 46:1—"God is my refuge and strength, a very present help in trouble"—and in Revelation 1:8—"I am the Alpha and Omega, the beginning and the ending, saith the Lord, which is and which was, and which is to come; the Almighty." With Him, everything falls in place. I am greatly enthralled and highly favored, as I find comfort in the knowledge that my God, the supreme ruler of the universe, is not only on my side but also in control.

- I seek to appreciate all of God's creation, as I demonstrate love for God and humankind in all I do. This paired principle—showing unconditional love for God and unwavering love for my fellow humans—informs my conduct and defines my spirituality. I unrelentingly strive to show love for God and individuals, with the resultant obligation of treating others as I want to be treated.

God's creation of human beings and the universe is one of the most vivid manifestations of God's love for us. It is a model of love that I must seek to emulate. His love for each of us is further manifested in His gift of His only begotten Son (John

3:16), as He enjoins us to love one another. Therefore, I commit to be generous with service and friendliness, though frugal with friendship.

Of necessity, I am obliged not only to love God but also to fear his awe-inspiring attributes, keep His commandments, and seek righteousness. My spirituality (or relationship with Him) is revealed on two planes: (1) through prayer, praise, and worship, which reflects my vertical relationship with God, and (2) in my actions, as evinced in my horizontal relationships with persons, things, and ideas. Through actions of love and godliness, I manifest my divine nature and showcase the divinity that resides in me.

- Seek diligently to know the world and understand the Word.

My constant preoccupation is learning about God and acquiring useful knowledge about the environment. To live meaningfully in the world, one must know the world; to live by the Word, one must practice the Word. To love and serve God, one must understand Him. Knowing involves acquiring knowledge, whereas understanding requires establishing a relationship through action and collaboration. Profound knowledge about God and a close relationship with God are attained only through study and contemplation. Learning about God, therefore, requires dedicated moments of contemplation for deep intimacy with God and His attributes.

As a follower of Christ, I am admonished in 2 Timothy 2:15–16 "to study and show myself approved unto God, a workman that needeth not to be ashamed, rightly dividing the word of truth. But shun profane and vain babblings: for they will increase unto more ungodliness." Therefore, I strive to study the Word with the understanding that divine intervention is legitimately claimed only by those who understand God and have developed a personal relationship with Him.

A proper understanding of God and a deep knowledge of my environment enable me to cultivate an enlightened self-knowledge that is aligned with my self-defined purpose in life. To embrace and fully appreciate the greatness and vastness of God and nature, humility without self-deprecation is essential. Thus, the world unmistakably becomes a projection and amplification of my self-knowledge. My knowledge of self and of my external world provide the springboard from which I comprehend, model, and reify my conception of the supreme being.

I strive to seize almost every opportunity to study the Word, as well as to build a relationship with my God as I seek to know this world and the universe. I relentlessly strive for deeper knowledge and understanding of God, myself, and the world around me. Such knowledge and practice are extracted from the Bible and other books of faith, as well as from literature in the liberal arts and sciences. I believe I cannot love God unless I acquire a deep understanding of Him. To love God requires knowing Him first and then understanding Him. To understand Him involves learning about Him and developing a relationship with His attributes as well as with Him. The greatest book of my faith instructs me to "seek the Kingdom of God above all else, and live righteously, and He will give everything I need" (Matthew 6:33).

Bearing in mind that ignorance undercuts my divine attributes, I aspire to acquire and utilize the necessary knowledge, skills, and attitude to manage the vicissitudes of life. The use of all of my human senses in this endeavor is crucial. Certainly, when knowledge is adequately acquired and appropriately employed, it can be a reliable tool and useful resource for personal adaptation and social reconstruction. I whisper the constant refrain to myself: to understand my place and role in varied contexts and events, I will constantly aspire to acquire and use an elevated and refined self-knowledge for righteous and selfless living.

- I commit to translating knowledge of God and of the world into purpose and actions for daily living. Though knowledge about the world and the Word is a potential resource, it becomes useful only when it is practiced. I embrace the realization that knowledge of God, the world, and self, as well as of my relationship with the totality of my environment, is indispensable to cultivating a healthy balance and peaceful coexistence with my world. As vital as it is, knowledge is only useful in its employ.

The Bible admonishes us to "be doers of the word, and not merely hearers who deceive themselves … For if anyone is a hearer of the word and not a doer, he is like a man observing his natural face in a mirror; for he observes himself, goes away, and immediately forgets what kind of man he was" (James 1:22–24).

I strive to use knowledge acquired through purposeful study about God and the universe to consistently inform and shape my thoughts, my speech, and my actions. In order to work toward banishing ignorance and deepening my knowledge and understanding of God, myself, and my temporal world, I commit to reading voraciously, participating in constructive discussions, and rigorously and unrelentingly exercising my mind.

In the same vein, understanding and interacting meaningfully with my environment involves not only familiarity with the totality of its content but also seeking to maintain harmony with all that is naturally contained therein. As an integral part of my environment, I constantly strive to maintain my balance with it. In order to nourish and maintain a healthy physical body, I endeavor to eat well, sleep adequately, and engage in physical exercise daily. At the same time, I practice moderation in thought, word, and deed. Useful knowledge about self is translated into harmonious interaction with others. My commitment to building and utilizing a rich knowledge base is reflected in all aspects of my dealings with the world.

- Show due respect for God, humankind, and all of God's creation, but fear no one.

In everything I do, I acknowledge and act in the knowledge of the awesome nature and capacity of God. I find support in the Word, as stipulated in the book of Proverbs. "In all thy ways acknowledge Him and He shall direct your paths" (Proverbs 3:6). I strive to shape my conduct as well as my physical and social environment, according to the Word, by demonstrating respect for all of God's creation. Above all, I seek to be cordial to all human beings, even as I nurture selective friendships (deliberately and particularly with persons who can complement my character, supplement my aspirations, and reinforce my divine nature).

In addition to learning to love and respect every human being, it behooves me to equally love all of God's creation, including the flora and fauna. Because I seek to love my fellow human beings, I treat everyone as I want to be treated. Likewise, as a good steward of nature's bounteous content, I use the abundant resources of Mother Earth sparingly and responsibly, in the high hope of bequeathing them to posterity, pure, wholesome, and unsullied. To cultivate and fortify the essence of my spirituality, I seek to maintain constant communication with God through prayer, studying, fasting, and contemplation on the things of God. In the final analysis, I align myself with the disposition to surrender myself and my all to God.

Naturally, I fear no one. Though the actions or character traits of a person may evoke fear or trepidation, I have learned never to submit to fear of one's personhood. I do entertain the belief that, though the fear of the Lord is the beginning of wisdom (Proverbs 1:7), the fear of humankind stifles personal growth, locks up creativity, and retards or extinguishes self-actualization.

- Subdue improper passions and compete with none but self.

Uncontrolled human emotions and passions are the usual sources of human anguish. Improper passion can inflict anguish on the perpetrator as well as the victim. Passion that is shrouded in uncontrolled or extreme emotions (such as anger, hatred, greed, love) is self-destructive and improper. Human disquietude is usually a product of one or a combination of improper passions associated with hate, arrogance, deceit, or anxiety caused by impatience, greed, or envy. Improper passions often manifest themselves as vices with dysfunctional effects. To be passionate about a person, an object, or an event is to be driven primarily by that person or thing, usually at the expense of reasoning or uprightness. As a counterforce, temperance is a valued ally. In efforts to exercise moderation and self-control, I aim to satisfy my survival needs, reduce my sundry wants, subdue my passions, and avoid excess in all I do or say. Deliberately, I seek to subject my passions to reasoning and righteousness, for untamed desires and wants lead to overly agitated passions and self-destructive conduct. I should not undertake actions and conduct that are not subordinate to reasoning and righteousness. My practical commitment to acts of self-restraint, though far from being perfect, provides me with a blueprint for peaceful daily living.

In every stage of my life, I have identified my yardstick and set my personal goals. Even before the end of my third year at the Prince of Wales Secondary School, I had envisaged being a professional in academia and equipping myself with an academic degree. It was my ambition from an early age to seek to improve the human condition through education and training. I deliberately avoided copying others as the yardstick of my progress and development. I have always maintained that I am divinely and uniquely created. My path to self-actualization is uniquely mine. I entertain no doubt that, any attempt at duplicating others would rob me of my uniqueness and originality. Also, investing my limited human resources in imitating others is one sure measure to deprive me of the requisite focus and attention for perfecting my unique qualities and reaching my full potential. Seeking to imitate others would not only prevent me from attaining my unique best but also could foster dysfunctional relationships with others. Unhealthy rivalry and competition that is geared toward outdoing or outperforming others often breeds disunity, jealousy, and antagonism. Usually, it generates unhealthy personal and social relationships that can threaten peace.

Summarizing my Guiding Principles

I doubtlessly believe that the guiding principles I have established will amply equip me to face difficult or defining events in life with the requisite knowledge, conviction, and spiritual fortitude. In addition, they will continue to guide my evolution and support me with a sound and enlightened mind in a healthy body. These principles are a product of contemplation. They are the contemplative products of an array of significant incidences and life-changing events. These events have profoundly impacted my life and altered my belief system. They represent a formative cluster of events that have necessitated some of the most profound occurrences of introspection and retrospection. The guiding principles provide a reasoned framework for making rational choices and generating measured reactions to problems and situations in life. They have shaped my past and dictated the present, as they launched me into the future.

Life-Changing Challenges and Personal Bouts with Turmoil

From time to time, we encounter life-changing challenges that can either make or break us. The challenges and circumstances, as well as the duration, sequence, and intensity of their influence on us may vary from individual to individual. For some, the life-changing events may be the loss of a loved one or a relationship, marriage-related chasms, financial or legal challenges, health or job-related anguish, inter-family or intra-family conflict and rivalry, or the like. As for me, these challenges were events that tested the depth of my courage and the strength of my deeply held convictions. While exposing my frailties and nothingness before God, these challenges forced me into serious contemplation and sustained meditation. I found much truth in the assertion that hardship or difficult moments build character. The rigor of those experiences not only made a lasting impression on my outlook but also significantly aided me in defining my purpose in life. The six defining moments and life-changing events that follow are acutely significant and worthy of citation.

My Life-Changing and Defining Events

My personal bouts with turmoil were accentuated by varied life-changing events. These events not only toughened me but also shaped my perspectives on my existence and defined the trajectory of my life. The following six event summaries provide the context of some of my most potentially destabilizing challenges and bouts with turmoil.

- The premature drowning of hope: This narrative depicts the death by drowning of a college mate and dear friend, Ade W.
- Learning to know me: This episode reveals my internalization of the death of my father, Edward Prince Nicol.
- Testing the waters by diving into the unfamiliar: The narrative describes pivotal events that defined my sojourn in Côte d'Ivoire.
- Self-transplanting for self-renewal: The episode examines my relocating to the US and the resultant soul-searching for the essence of my existence.
- Piloting the vessel through a tempest: The narrative highlights the challenge of managing and maintaining sanity in a middle school in the nation's capital amid the 9/11 turmoil.
- Losing a soul mate among soulless mates: This episode narrates the devastating personal loss of my dear wife, Leo.

The peaks and valleys in life provide opportunities for some to soar like an eagle and for others to burrow into oblivion like the cicada. Many more barely survive them. In an effort to provide context to the life-changing events depicting my personal challenges and bouts with turmoil, I furnish the following summary, highlighting the major events of each of six episodes.

The Premature Drowning of Hope

This episode contextualizes the death by drowning of a college mate and dear friend at the Milton Margai Teachers College. Before entering college, Ade and I barely knew each other and had only interacted briefly and casually on a couple of occasions in Waterloo. Nonetheless, the two of us had a lot in common. Like him, I entered college at the age of eighteen. Like me, Ade hailed from Waterloo. Like him, our respective families frequently spent the three major yearly school holidays in Waterloo. Like me, Ade was nurtured in a God-fearing Christian home.

My first sustained and meaningful interaction with Ade occurred during our first couple of days on campus. Following dinner in the main dining hall, scores of first-year students congregated in random numbers and in varied proximity to the main entrance of the dining hall. A towering plum tree, conspicuously located halfway between the men's and women's hostels and roughly at midpoint between the Great Hall and the dining hall, furnished inviting shade and a strategic location for informal student gatherings. Fortuitously, Ade and I met there and exchanged a few pleasantries. With cordiality and unguarded familiarity, we shared our residence hall room numbers and locations. Also, with unspoken accord and unanimity, we shared the shade of that plum tree. Shortly thereafter, we were deeply engrossed in conversations of mutual interest of a personal nature.

As first-year students, we discussed a commitment to orienting ourselves to key locations and premium campus activities. From our vantage point, Ade and I silently observed a bevy of young women, some of the most delightful and beautiful on campus. Unabashedly, we demonstrated an atypical keenness to meet, greet, and engage a few of them in brief strands of socialization. Ade and I were also quick to discover that our interests, when not identical, were similar. With a burning desire to achieve academically, Ade and I were bonded by shared academic ambition as well as similar religious and socio-cultural interests. By the end of that first week of college, our conclave grew in number from two and three to four and then six. Kenneth, a childhood friend and elementary and secondary school mate, had deeply buried ancestral roots in Waterloo. Naturally, Kenneth was a member of our original conclave of three. Sigismund, Titus, and Henry later joined us. We ate together, studied together, attended religious services together, traveled to and from downtown together, and did almost everything else together. In practice, we replicated home-based brotherhood away from home, and each of us stood in the gap as each other's brother's keeper on campus. Whenever we were together, almost every event turned out to be fun.

Furtively, the academic year sped past us. The year's end drew nigh. Then, the end-of-year final exams were upon us. The exam schedule informally dictated how fast any lost ground had to be recovered. It was time for us to account for those endless moments of reckless partying and jubilant celebrations. The exam schedule also reminded us of those wasted evenings in the student commons and student union canteen. There, we had serially played chess, checkers, draughts, or Ludo and gulped bottles of Guinness, Heineken, and Star beer. With a silent but justified cry for accountability, the exam schedule dictated that we could no longer recklessly indulge in intemperate activities. Also, loosely accommodating overnight visitors was no longer an attractive option. The focus on academics, once again, assumed prominence.

The most intimidating test of academic rigor and endurance on campus was in educational psychology and educational measurement and evaluation (also known as educational statistics). Both subdisciplines were under the tutelage of the most dreaded and the most academically demanding lecturer on campus. College records would suggest that some of the highest rates of failure, academic references, and expulsions from campus originated from those two subdisciplines. Without doubt, those two subcategories presented the greatest threats to our graduation from college. With justified trepidation and rigorous preparation, we readied ourselves for the much dreaded and talked about exam in educational psychology and statistics. On the day of the exam, with focused attention on each question, I spent the better part of the allotted three or so hours answering the questions. The exam, however, turned out to be a pleasant surprise.

Astoundingly, I walked out of the exam hall believing that the much-talked-about rigidity of the exam was a farcical exaggeration of rigor. Soon thereafter, Sigismund walked out, immediately followed by Henry, Kenneth, Ade, and Titus. We all came out of the exam hall with heightened optimism, convinced that some form of celebration was in place. We appeared to have felt good about our individual performances. Only time would tell. So we resolved to wait for the results with confident anticipation of success.

Meanwhile, with unanimous consent and without debate, we opted to go to the beach to have some fun. We dashed into the physical education room and selected a couple of soccer balls for a football match in celebration of our much-anticipated success on the exam. As a bonus, we would also enjoy the peace-inspiring breezes and waves of the Atlantic Ocean.

With playful exuberance, the conclave of six (Ade, Kenneth, Sigismund, Titus, Henry, and I) headed for the beach. Less than thirty minutes later, we had begun a full-fledged soccer match on the sandy beach of Founkya. For the next couple of hours, we laughed, poked fun at each other, and joked. We played soccer until the distant sun began to conceal some of its colorful beauty behind the inflexible rim of the horizon. With silent unanimity, we reached the conclusion that it was time to end play and return to campus. We then rinsed off the sand from our bodies with a brief dip in the shallow waters. One after the other, we walked away from the shallow edges of the coastline toward the sandy shore. Ade, being the last to attempt to leave the water, hesitantly stopped. He asked the rest of us to count off the seconds to determine how long he could stay underwater. For a while, he held on to the soccer ball, as he stayed partially afloat. He then dove into the chest-deep water of the Atlantic.

Titus kept count – 10, 20, 30, 40, 50, — while the rest of us participated in some other distraction. After the count of 360 or so, my attention was drawn to Titus' utterance and stupor, "Where is Ade?" In the blink of an eye, the once-friendly water of the beach seemed to have transformed into a raging and temperamental beast. With the ball still afloat at the shoreline, the now bestial water gave no clue of Ade's whereabouts. Panic, shrouded in paralyzing fear, set in. I briefly entertained the idea of going back to the spot where I last saw Ade, but I dreaded venturing into the now-raging ocean one more time. We yelled and summoned the assistance of the local fishermen, who had cast their fishing nets a few hundred meters from where we were. The next few minutes seemed like hours, and the wait for Antipa, the renowned local fisherman and famed diver, seemed to last eternally. In the interim, the local fishermen engaged in the search and rescue. Each passing moment reinforced my suspicion that we had lost Ade for good. My rejection of that suspicion, tainted with ambivalence, was serially persistent.

As the news of Ade's drowning spread like wildfire, the pool of self-promoted interviewers and investigators swelled. Each asked what had happened and how it happened. Increasing numbers of beachfront residents, students in the vicinity, townsfolk, and bystanders jammed the scene. One of the final-year students came close enough to me and whispered, "Do you know it is a violation of college rules for you to have left campus without the consent of the college resident director?"

Another asked, "Do you know you can be suspended or even expelled from college for that?"

If true, what a drastic change in fortune! What a rude awakening and sharp contrast to the original jubilant exclamation that heralded us onto the beach. I realized we were in serious trouble.

My misery soared with each passing moment. Confounded and perturbed, I attempted to process a few questions that raced through my mind: Will the college authorities suspend or expel us? Will we be saved this evening by a miracle? How can prayer save us? Will we see Ade again? If so, will it be too late for Ade's cardiac resuscitation? Why didn't we urge him to come ashore instead of agreeing to his request for a final dive? How are we going to explain this tragedy to our parents? How will Ade's parents react to the news of his drowning?"

To add salt to my emotional wound, I could hear a siren and see the flashing lights of a police vehicle approaching in the distance. It seemed like my world stood still as the vehicle sped toward me. I was as paralyzed with fear as I was stunned by the over-run of events. The Land Rover pulled up with two police officers on the two front seats. The driver asked us—the remaining five of the original six—to identify ourselves. Following the verification of our identity, the driver unlocked the tailgate and ushered us into the rear compartment of the Land Rover. Like an escaped prisoner resuming police custody, each of us mounted the vehicle without knowing our destination or our fate. The ride took us through the sandy trails of the beach, then through Campus Drive, and finally to the Registrar's Office. The ten- to fifteen-minute ride was as rough and bumpy as the wretched emotions it evoked.

We were escorted into the office and then subsequently taken for individual interrogation. With marked politeness and congeniality, the police officers scrupulously embarked on their fact-finding mission. Separately, they bombarded each of us with questions. The group interrogation, which ended on a much friendlier note, followed immediately thereafter. Unfortunately, neither our meeting with the registrar nor the interrogation by the police officers provided any assurance to me that all questions pertaining to Ade's drowning had been satisfactorily answered. What would happen next remained unknown. My fear and discomfort associated with that uncertainty lingered painfully. Still, I could not fathom the idea that when all was said and done, Ade seemed to have gone for good.

I could not reckon with such a premature death of a buddy so full of energy, promise, and goodness. Most excruciating to me was the realization that I had permanently lost a town's mate and a true friend. It quickly dawned on me that I might never again find a friend so real, so simple, and so dependable. Ade was gifted with so many great qualities. To have known him was to have wedded to kindness and congeniality. Generosity and probity were uniquely his unrivaled strengths. I never knew him to lie to me or to any other member of the conclave. His exercise of self-control was so impressive and enticing. To get along with him was as common place as his random acts of generosity and casual frankness. As for his laughs, they could be heard and recognized from a distance beyond sight. Not even the discovery of his cadaver three days later, scores of miles away, could convince me that he would be with us no more.

Nonetheless, I was tormented by countless unanswered questions and unresolved discrepancies: Why should Ade die so young? What could we have done to prevent Ade's death, and where did we go wrong? Why should Ade's' parents be put through such agony? I asked myself, "Can the unbridled power of death rupture our existence, even when we are at the zenith of our strength?"

A potpourri of thoughts about my mortality overwhelmed my consciousness, as I pondered the inevitability and brutality of death. Little did I know then that another imminent death would once more compel me to probe even deeper into my self-knowledge and purpose-driven existence. The currency of time began to feature prominently in my thoughts about my temporary and temporal existence. Perplexed and often mesmerized by the persistent and dominant thought of Ade's demise, I continued my determined efforts to complete my schooling promptly, without interruption or failure of any kind. Time was of the essence, as I contended with what seemed to be Ade's untimely death. Knowing me better was the process, and defining a purpose emerged as the product.

The following episode – Learning to know me — depicts the internalization of another death—that of my father.

Learning to Know Me

Learning to know me reveals my continued search for my true identity. It also depicts the shock, internalization, and acceptance of the death of my earthly father. It's a peek into the context of my father's physical existence, his indomitable influence on me and the family, and finally, my perception of him up to and after his physical demise. The episode ushered in a period of self-knowledge that dictated the road map for the rest of my life. The cumulative experiences of antecedent events, including my sustained and expansive interaction with my father, proved invaluable. These experiences facilitated the construction of a blueprint that would guide me through the intricate windings of my mortal existence.

My father's physical demise occurred at the end of my second year in college, long after the indelible early-morning walk at Lumley Beach. Almost a year after Ade's drowning, the final exams approached again. Like the year before, the weeks preceding final exams uncovered an unexplained but significant unease in my daily routine. For no apparent reason, a stale atmosphere of somberness enveloped my world. It seemed to mark the coming of doom and gloom.

Barely three weeks before the beginning of the final exams, I made the usual weekend trip home. That trip was intended to amass food and money—two resources that would normally come in handy during and after exams. It proved to be one of those restful weekends, of which the Sunday morning church service was the sole highlight. By mid afternoon, I had assembled every food item that my tote could carry in preparation for my return trip to campus. After bidding me farewell, my mother pulled me aside and affectionately handed me her relatively modest pecuniary donation toward my weekly campus expenses. My dad, who was usually the last to hand me his, was frequently a more generous giver. I waited patiently for the slightest indication from him that he was ready to send me to his safe. Being his most trusted errand boy, I knew he would rely on me to fetch him the specific money bag from which he would hand me my much-anticipated allowance or pocket money.

Papa, as we affectionately called my father, finally directed me to fetch him the money bag—the main event that truly had initially prompted my visit home. His directives to me bore the precise location of the safe, as well as the exact corner and color of the money bag. Within seconds, I had found the bag and handed it to him with pretentious indifference. He took out an unspecified sum of money and asked me to return the bag to the safe. Not long after returning from the safe, I picked up my tote before saying goodbye. After his customary brief counseling session, we prayed, and then he handed me my allowance for the remainder of the semester. He reinforced his expectations for me and counseled me to continue to be good and hardworking.

As I went through the usual protocol preceding physical separation from my parents, I reiterated that we barely had three weeks of college work to end the academic year. I walked across the veranda and headed for the metal egress gate. I turned around to steal a glance at my father and found him doing the same to me. I walked away slowly with unexplained reluctance, as if I knew that was my last glimpse of Papa. I had always treasured how lucky I was to be the product of such exemplary parents. I could not help but nurture even greater love, appreciation, and esteem for them.

In each of my interactions with my father, I literally found some justification to love him more, respect him more, appreciate him more, and even seek to emulate him more. To me, he was among the finest specimens of a disciplined mind and orderly lifestyle; an inspiring example of pure altruism, a true model of an encyclopedic intellect, and a stout icon of exemplary moral rectitude. Papa was an exceptionally loving and responsible father, a respected and respectable citizen, and above all, he was law-abiding and godly. I never knew him to tell or promote a lie. He was never known to have used vulgarity or profanity. He never exhibited intemperance of any sort. One of his most impressive qualities was that he paid rapt attention to his fatherly obligations. Papa never ignored or trivialized the needs and reasonable wants of his family. Never did I find him wanton in his responsibility as head of the household. He led by example and loathed being the subject of begging, borrowing, stealing, or deceit. In brief, he was the best father I ever knew. He could be ranked second only to my mother in his love for, commitment to, and pride in his children. Saying goodbye to either of them, however fleeting or temporary, was an agonizing exercise.

With mixed feelings on that Sunday, I waved goodbye to both of them, comforted by the apparent certainty of seeing them in a couple of weeks. Slowly, I walked away like a ship sailing away from port into unknown waters. I arrived on campus late that Sunday evening, too exhausted to entertain any of the two floating proposals to join either of two campus study groups that evening. Tired yet emboldened by the knowledge that I had never experienced failure in any major exam, I chose to relax. I reckoned that three weeks of rigorous studying, all by myself, would be sufficient to make up for all the time wasted during the academic year. I privately committed to going solo, revving all cylinders and studying in earnest, starting the next evening. A peaceful rest was, therefore, as necessary as it was deserved.

The events of the following evening unfolded uneventfully. The after-dinner groups of students stippled the verdant lawns adorning Campus Drive. Not even that colorful and artful display of students could tempt me to spare another minute from my study time. I hastened to my room, picked up my books and other study materials, and headed for my cherished French language lecture hall. I secured my usual isolated corner, where I was intent on studying for the rest of the evening and the better part of the early-morning hours. In the first couple of hours, I breezed through a couple of textbooks and my handwritten notes. I soon felt comfortably confident that I was meeting (if not exceeding) the anticipated levels of comprehension and retention. That silky flow of progress was abruptly halted by Henry's brusque appearance. His uncommon insistence that he had looked practically everywhere for me, coupled with his stern advice that I should report to the main office without delay, was as troubling to me as his insistence that I take all my books with me. I asked myself, "Is Henry serious, or is he joking? What is the reason for this all-important summons to the main office?

Did I do or say anything wrong or inappropriate on campus? Is my family okay?"

The dash from the lecture hall to the main office lasted an eternity. Meanwhile, my mind strayed agonizingly from one sinister possibility to another. Immediately upon my arrival at the office, the receptionist calmly instructed me to pick up the telephone in the secretary's office. I picked up the phone. On the other end of the line was my older brother, Wachuku. First, he prepped me for the once-in-a-lifetime news by extolling my unfeigned maturity into manhood.

"You are now a man, aren't you?" he asked. Then, he slowly spilled the most painful news I had ever heard. "Papa died suddenly this evening of a heart attack."

In disbelief, I dropped the phone on the floor. Dumbfounded, numbed, and fizzled, my world froze.

Although there could have been no better source of obtaining the dreaded news than from my brother, disbelief swayed me toward naked optimism. "That cannot be true," I insisted. The fear of confronting the reality of Papa's demise paralyzed me. Temporarily, I sought shelter in the thought that it could be a mistake or a joke, for nature could not be so unkind! To assuage my doubts, I needed some confirmation of the news. It seemed as if my incredulity could only be reversed by sight. Ocular verification and joining the rest of the family were the two best options for neutralizing my doubts and disbelief. Making a trip home that evening was a time-sensitive necessity. I sprinted to my room, packed my bag, and in less than fifteen minutes, I was ready to embark on the trip home.

Shortly before midnight, I left campus for what I believed would be my longest trip home. Thanks to the talkative disposition of Sigismund who kindly offered to escort me home, the journey proved less tedious and excruciating than I'd anticipated. On arrival at the family residence, I could see the atypical movement of people and the solemnity with which they conducted themselves. That unwelcoming sight confirmed my original suspicion and negated all hopes that nothing abnormally grave had befallen my family. It affirmed the currency that something macabre had taken place. My mother, who was the first to acknowledge that morbid homecoming, greeted me with tearful cries, "Your dad is gone!" That was the second time I had seen my mother shed tears; the first was when her mother, Mama Yo, passed. My eyes slowly started to tear, and then like a torrent, I began to weep profusely and bitterly. Was I weeping because I'd seen my mother weep? Did I weep because Papa was gone, or was my weeping in recognition of my own mortality and subsequent fatality?

In truth, I could not think of life without my father. He was the umbrella sheltering the family and protecting us all from the ravages of life. As an inseparable duo with my mother, he was the fountain of domestic authority, the generous sustainer of my well-being. In collaboration with my mother, he was my earthly provider and the most potent source of inspiration. His standing in the community was exemplary, his service to others was praiseworthy, and his striving for righteousness was persistent. We basked in the trails he'd blazed and were uplifted by the positive energy gleaned from his reputation. To me, Papa was not only irreplaceable but also inimitable. His death created a physical, mental, and social abyss. "Will recovery from this loss ever be surmountable?" I repeatedly asked myself.

Edward Nicol was not only my moral compass but also the rudder that gave direction to my life. To me, he was the most dependable depot of knowledge about God, humankind, and the world. His death forced me, for the first time, to confront my own mortality. Papa's death brought me closer to entertaining the thought that each day of life was a day in preparation for death. It made me wonder whether death was truly the inevitable destiny of all humans. Further, it obliged me to pose the following questions: Can death eternally isolate our loved ones from us and disrupt our temporal plans at will? Should we accept the overwhelming power of death, or can we alter the time and mode of our own mortal demise? Is death permanently irreversible?

The brutal finality of death, the uncertainty of the time of its call, and the biting brusqueness of its clutches plunged me into perpetual thinking and unease. The death of Papa demolished my comfort zone and ruptured my sense of security.

Looking back, I realize that the impetus to discover myself stemmed from the unease that Papa's demise had caused me. It not only forced me to contemplate my own mortality but also to plot a purpose for my temporal existence. The unanticipated passing of my father charged me with continuing his legacy and seeking to perpetuate those fine qualities that had ennobled his life and memorialized his existence. After Papa's death, the lessons learned from him were transformed into an unspoken mandate and a charge to leave the world a better place than I'd found it. His death gave birth to my burning desire to improve on my condition with a view to improving the human condition. As much as it disturbed my peace, my father's death led me into contemplation. Also, it empowered me and propelled me into an unknown future that was convincingly pregnant with possibilities.

As I sought to discover myself and reach my full potential, I progressed in age, experience, and academic refinement. I attained a noteworthy milestone soon after my twenty-first birthday. I was summoned to the French embassy in Freetown to receive one of five national post-graduation bursaries for advanced studies in French language, literature, and pedagogy at the University of Grenoble in France. That experience whetted my appetite for future studies abroad. I returned from France convinced that I had a constructive role in public education, particularly in improving teaching and learning at the secondary or tertiary level.

Testing the Waters by Diving into the Unfamiliar

Testing the waters by diving into the unfamiliar refers to my relocation and sojourn in Côte d'Ivoire. Diving into unfamiliar waters summoned me to act on faith. Echoing the author, John Ortberg's assertion, I felt enjoined to comply with his call to action, "If you want to walk on water, you've got to get out of the boat" (Ortberg 2001). By faith, I engaged in the bold and risky undertaking of relocating to the Côte d'Ivoire. My relocation would be my first attempt at independent living. It would engender a lifestyle devoid of the protection and sponsorship of my parents or their surrogate. Having embraced the conviction that I could leave home at will, I was rattled by the reality of actualizing the plan. Giving up the familiarity of my social circle, the warmth and coziness of my home, the predictability of family love, and the ready and prompt needs-based intervention of friends and family soon proved to be abundantly unattractive. To surrender the known (with its known incentives and disincentives) for the unknown (even with its potential for endless possibilities) became somehow logically indefensible.

After serious self-examination and careful assessment of the available options, I settled for Côte d'Ivoire (or Ivory Coast, as she was then called) as my exit point to France. Subsequently, the more I learned about the Ivory Coast, the stronger my conviction grew that Abidjan was my launch pad to Europe. The reality of never having set foot on Ivorian soil was not strong enough to dissuade me from setting my plan in motion

Frightening thoughts accented the sleepless nights preceding my departure for Abidjan. Fear soon eased into the void occasioned by ignorance, as the power of my powerlessness dominated my thoughts and actions. I shuddered then to accept the disturbing reality that I had only one sure contact in the Ivory Coast. The scanty details of his whereabouts were equally alarming. Leaving the comfort of my home was indeed no undertaking for the fainthearted. To walk away from the place of my birth and infant nurture, much more to say goodbye to those nearest and dearest to me, proved to be debilitating. Hugging my mother as I said goodbye to her proved to be my most excruciating experience associated with parting. Faced with the quandary, I asked myself, "Is this a fatal error?"

As I left the comfort of my home, I pondered over the emptiness of my decision to give up my family, my job, my students, my friends and relatives, and even my familiar environment. I asked myself, "Is the errant search for my artificial paradise and life's hidden treasure only a daydream and an adventure in futility?" Even with the luxury of hindsight, I felt justified in believing that it was one of the most unreasonable and least rational decisions of my life. After careful assessment, I felt it was a decision only a desperate person would make. In certitude, I was not that desperate! Meanwhile, my arrival in Abidjan on that sunny Wednesday was met with the warmth and glimmer of the tropical sun at its meridian.

Without regret, though, relocating to Abidjan proved to be a uniquely bold and consequential decision; one that ended in strengthening my spirituality and bringing me closer to my God. The fear of failure, the threats embedded in novelty, and the uncertainty associated with the availability of food, shelter, and clothing were a constant source of perturbation and turmoil. My wretched circumstance compelled me to summon the last vestiges of my faith and inner strength. I remember vividly that it was during this period that I read the Bible from cover to cover. Of necessity, I elevated praying and reading the Bible to a level of inviolable consistency for self-preservation, supplication, divine protection, and daily sustenance. I was quick to learn that even fools would seek intimacy with God when haunted by the overwhelming shadow of death or the agony of extreme hardship. The challenge of ensuring my survival and livelihood, maintaining my sanity, and seeking to stay within the bounds of propriety was addressed through supplication, contemplation, and prayerful action.

Relocating to Côte d'Ivoire launched me into a larger theater of the world, where my acquired knowledge, training, and experience would be put to the test. It exposed me to the novelty and challenges of a new and neutral environment, where I could define and launch the beginning of the rest of my life. Its neutrality offered me a fresh start, as I abandoned the intimate and predictable comfort of my past. Yes, it was destabilizing, but it would later prove to be promising.

The first year of my sojourn in Côte d'Ivoire was accentuated by the confounding challenge of identifying the normal and normalizing the abnormal. The period marked a voluntary commitment to sacrificing the common for the unique, the habitual for the abnormal, and the known for the unknown. It tasked me with making continuous adjustments to apparent changes in the external environment of people, things, and ideas. More often than not, these adjustments proved foreign, untested, and unique. The lone building block of stability and familiarity in my life was my faith in God, coupled with the hope of His timely and benign intervention.

The semblance of stability that my faith provided was savagely tested halfway into my first year in Côte d'Ivoire. My job search in Abidjan had netted only one job interview, which, by my assessment, was the only lifesaving opportunity. The verbal promise of the principal that confirmed my appointment as a teacher of English was both comforting and reassuring. I savored the imminence of commencing a teaching assignment at College VH in Abidjan at the beginning of the ensuing school year. With confident anticipation, I cherished the promise of resuming the respectable luxury of earning a living. In addition to the respect of being gainfully employed, the appointment would provide a much-needed boost to my nearly depleted financial resources. Above all, it would enable me to renew my immigrant visa for Côte d'Ivoire. Almost everything I could say or do (such as relocating from the hotel, regular source of food, clothing, etc.) depended on my having a job. I counted the weeks, days, and hours to the reopening of school.

About three weeks before the reopening of school, I gleefully visited the principal of College VH to lay hands on the formal contract, classroom assignment, teaching schedule, and the like. Then, to my great surprise, I was exposed to the wicked pangs of disappointment. The hopes of landing that teaching appointment were dashed few seconds into my discussion with the principal, when he casually reneged on his commitment. He feigned ignorance about the details of my previous visit and pretended to have forgotten either the details of the interview or the substance of his original job offer. My attempts to remind him of our previous relevant discussions were carelessly dismissed with stoic indifference. Dumbfounded and not knowing what my next action should be, I walked away in bewilderment, never to return to that principal's office.

Shrouded in despair and confusion, I sensed that thinking straight had now become more of a challenge than I ever anticipated. In addition, the sweltering heat from the midday rays of the tropical sun pelted my bare scalp. My decision to go home via Plateau by bus so I could ponder my limited options emerged as a priority. The bus arrived half full. On my return trip home, for no clear reason, I was impelled to make an unscheduled stop in downtown Plateau. Living in persistent uncertainty in Abidjan without a job could no longer be an inviting option. The emergent possibility of going back to Sierra Leone slowly became less far-fetched or repulsive. With evident vacillation, I opted to make a brief stop in the center of town with the hope of regrouping psychologically.

It seemed as if I would never recover from the shock of the principal's shameless display of dishonesty or incompetence. The disappointment was awe-inspiring, and the chances of obtaining another job interview before school reopened were remote. Nevertheless, I knew I should let go of that which was past and gone and be thankful for what I was left with, while confidently looking forward to what was yet to come. Strengthened by the Shakespearean admonition that what was done could not be undone, I resolved to succeed by fighting my battle with the sure power of prayer. Between stops, I would seriously invoke the mighty power of God, as I summoned His timely intervention in the affairs of my life.

Having no clear reason, objective, or mission, I alighted from the bus in downtown Plateau. Still weighing my limited options, I strolled through the city streets of Abidjan, believing that my days in Côte d'Ivoire were certainly numbered. From the bus stop, I aimlessly walked toward the Assemblée Nationale

(National Assembly Building) and up to the Stade Houphouet Boigny (Houphouet Boigny Soccer Stadium). Arriving in front of the Cour Suprême (Supreme Court Building), I found myself opposite the uniquely massive structure that housed the US Embassy. Curiosity led me through the main entrance and into the lobby, where I was greeted by the receptionist. No sooner had I concluded my formal greetings in French than the receptionist handed me a job application and a ballpoint pen. I painstakingly filled out the application form. With my body language manifesting my intent to wait in the lobby for the outcome of my application, I handed the completed application to the receptionist. He impressed upon me that the embassy would contact me by mail or telephone if the need arose.

I left the embassy somehow disappointed with my failure to earn an immediate interview but was partially upbeat and optimistic about the events of the day. I found great comfort in three of the four occurrences that had marked the major happenings of the day. The first occurrence—the principal's reneging on his original job offer—was the least pleasant. The second, which was my unscheduled stop in Plateau, gave rise to my unplanned visit to the US Embassy. Last but not least was the tendering of a completed application for employment.

That afternoon, I arrived home partially satisfied with the varied activities that signaled some movement in the right direction. The impetus thus created encouraged me to consider a second visit to the embassy before the end of that week to check on the status of my application. On that visit, after a courteous salutation in French, I inquired about the status of my application for employment. Without mincing words, the receptionist again advised me to go home and wait till I was called. Reluctantly, I walked away from the embassy lobby, sorely disappointed but convinced that I would imminently show up again at the embassy.

In exactly a week after my second visit to the embassy, I chose to return. Determined to find out what had happened to my application, I entered the lobby and walked straight to the receptionist. The receptionist again greeted me with a stern look. My question about the status of my application again resulted in the receptionist's usual instruction: "Sir, they would call you if they wanted to talk to you or offer you a job."

I insisted that I only wanted to know what had happened to the application I had submitted. With stern rejection, he advised me to go home and wait. I turned around and walked toward the exit but stopped to make a final appeal. Emboldened by desperation, I politely insisted on speaking with anybody from the Personnel Office who would listen to me. With obvious reluctance, the receptionist pointed to a phone in the lobby and asked me to dial extension 306 from it. I did so, and a female voice answered, asking, "How can I be of help to you?"

With the convincing pitch of a used-car salesman and with the speed of lighting, I gave the reason for my call, my qualifications and experience, and my potential usefulness to the embassy. After a brief dialogue, I was relieved when she remarked, "You sound interesting. I think I should meet with you in person. I'll send someone to escort you up to my office." That soothing voice, I later learned, was the voice of the personnel director herself. I also later learned that obtaining an unscheduled audience with the personnel director was as rare as her answering a telephone call from that extension. On that day, however, those two unlikely events merged into a pleasant reality.

In a couple of minutes, my escort arrived. Moments thereafter, I was on the fifth floor, face-to-face with the director herself. I knew I had only one opportunity to make a first impression. The interview that followed was exceedingly smooth. Without doubt, I felt I made a genial, enlightened, and lasting impression on her. Unfortunately, she was quick to confess that I was certainly overqualified for the available position. I calmly reassured her of my willingness to enter the organization at any point, confident that my work ethic and performance would determine, if not justify, my future career mobility. Before asking her secretary to escort me to the lobby, she informed me that she was considering slotting me in one of two potential vacancies under consideration. She asked me to come see her the next Thursday.

Feeling relieved, I gleefully walked out of the embassy with some optimism and assurance that the end of the dark tunnel might be in sight. My trip to the embassy that Thursday marked the beginning of the second phase of indelible life-changing experiences in Côte d'Ivoire. It was truly the turning point in my quest to immigrate to Europe. It also abruptly altered the trajectory of my desire to continue my studies in France. Before then, coming to America had neither been an attractive option for me nor under any active or serious consideration. On the contrary, acts in fortuity had dictated a series of remarkable detours that ended up reversing my thrust away from teaching.

Instead of aligning with public schools, I landed in the diplomatic service—from a local school to the US Embassy, and from France to the United States. What appeared to have been fortuitous events led me to the realization that man's disappointment (as with the principal of College VH) could certainly be an appointment with God's grace, mercy, and love. In addition, some of those unexplained occurrences eased me to the belief that my greatest accomplishments could be at the other side of my greatest fears.

Self-Transplanting for Self-Renewal

Self-transplanting for self-renewal describes my relocating to the United States and my soul-searching for the essence of my existence. Throughout my stay in Côte d'Ivoire, I embraced the conviction that continuing my formal education was my number-one priority. Therefore, all my efforts were choreographed to subsume this primary ambition.

My third year in Abidjan exposed me to a period of continued personal, social, and economic growth, with evident tokens of material prosperity. The comfort of social and economic stability was abundantly uplifting, if not euphoric. In addition, the demands of demonstrating competence in a bilingual position was personally rewarding and professionally stimulating. Though I enjoyed my work and sought excellence in my endeavors in the Ivory Coast, I did not lose sight of my personal goals. I had fun while I worked diligently. Not even four job promotions in three years could induce me to take my eyes off the prize. While holding fast to my job and treating it with utmost seriousness, I knew I had lots more to offer to society and humanity. I knew I had to address the parallel challenge of pursuing my academic ambition while seeking to excel at work. I was intensely driven by the untamed ambition of promptly attaining the apex of the academic pyramid by obtaining a terminal degree. Anything short of reaching that goal was a clear and uncontestable expression and admission of failure on my part.

Consequently, I committed to enrolling in independent studies at the University of Nebraska–Lincoln. I took some of the college advanced-placement exams in the consular office of the embassy, and I breezed through the coursework. After a couple of semesters, I became fully convinced that pursuing advanced studies in the United States was both feasible and plausible. My obligation to submit completed assignments fortnightly, though tedious at first, compelled me to reduce my social activities and subordinate my hedonistic instincts. Likewise, my decision to engage in savings for college via direct payroll deduction proved to be among the most empowering of my decisions. Soon, half of my biweekly salary regularly augmented my US-based bank savings account. Like the receipt of my monthly bank statement, the receipt of my graded or returned college work was both pleasing and reassuring.

Though my stay in Côte d'Ivoire exposed me to diverse opportunities and divers possibilities, I knew that I deserved a lot more for my personal, intellectual, and spiritual growth than Côte d'Ivoire could offer. I embraced the understanding that nothing short of an environment that was replete with robust opportunities for unbridled self-actualization would fully address my aspirations. My daily interaction with Americans at the embassy, my association with the American culture at work, and my closeness to them at social functions whetted my appetite for a deeper understanding and genuine appreciation of the American way. I discovered excitement in the novelty of the new and varied experience.

Still, my eye was on the prize. I ceaselessly reminded myself that I had left Sierra Leone with an uncompromised commitment to improving my capacity to make a dent in society. I was frequently reminded of my father's advice—that I owed it to myself to make me an able body first, en route to becoming a competent citizen later, for I can give my best only if and when I am at my best. I also maintained that it was better to be prepared for an opportunity and not have one than to have an opportunity and be unprepared for it. My priority was to acquire the requisite education and skills to enable me to achieve an optimal capacity for improving the human condition.

As my monetary savings grew and as my independent course credits accumulated, I became bolder in exploring college admission options. My bold efforts yielded great dividends when I received three acceptance letters by mail from three US universities within one week. It appeared that the foresight, commitment, and promise revealed in the results of my independent coursework provided college administrators a predictable assurance of future success. Armed with three college-admission offers and propped by a significant bank-savings statement, my ambition of immigrating to the United States for further studies was almost effortlessly realized.

The decision to relocate to the United States for further studies was a mixed bag of hope, courage, and tenacity. It was a revelation of bold determination propelled by strong conviction and dependable self-knowledge. Relocating to the US was certainly an expression of optimism that was doubly amplified by hope and of ambition transformed into action. This bold move was the condensed version of surrendering the known for the unknown. Leaving the relative stability of life in Abidjan, the familiarity with the culture, the tropical warmth, the proximity of Côte d'Ivoire to the land of my birth and infant nurture rendered the equation unbalanced.

Indubitably, leaving the shores of Freetown some four years earlier had been a terrifying undertaking. However, leaving the continent of Africa and venturing to the distant shores of the United States was a stretch of courage and a seemingly unjustified audacity of hope. The TV depiction of life in the US was my closest approximation of reality. It was a tapestry of reality that was laced with crime and violence, plagued with homicide, riddled with bullets, and renowned for unparalleled events of racism and racial tension. The commonplace scenes of man's inhumanity to man were all too vivid. The potential for me to be a victim of violence was intimidating and mind-boggling. Though I had definitely matured, my confidence in navigating the vast unknown was seriously unsettling. Fear of the unknown undermined my optimism, while my determination to succeed and my faith in God fueled my ambition. At the end of the day, the gentle hand of hope cuddled me toward the belief that all would be well.

Piloting the Vessel through a Tempest

Piloting the vessel through a tempest is my narrative on the governance of a school in the nation's capital as an island of stability during 9/11. The events in this episode unfolded more than two decades after my arrival in New York and subsequently at UN-Lincoln. About four years after my arrival at the academically stimulating and student-friendly university campus in Lincoln, I successfully concluded my third undergraduate and first graduate degrees with ease. No reason proved to be convincing enough to entice me to shy away from that less-traveled road paved with hard work, tenacity, and sacrifice. With undiluted focus on the prize and thousands of miles away from Nebraska, I boldly and contemporaneously vied for two more graduate degrees from a cherished and world-class research university in College Park, Maryland.

An impressive array of teaching experiences acquired at the University of Nebraska–Lincoln, Lincoln Office of Mental Retardation, as well as other public schools in Lincoln and Sierra Leone convinced me that I was poised for renewed and expanded professional responsibilities. Confident that I was ready to go toe-to-toe with other professionals in the highly competitive job market of the nation's capital, I planned to seek greener pastures in the Washington, DC, Metro area. Soon thereafter, my dream of reentering the teaching profession came to fruition. Resuming my career as a foreign-language teacher within months of my arrival in Washington, DC, was both professionally rewarding and personally uplifting.

As much as I enjoyed classroom teaching, I soon realized that the need for instructional and administrative leadership in the school system was copiously acute. In addition, my leadership and instructional expertise was systemically in much greater demand. Paradoxically, my yearning for a school-based administrative position was consistently and inexplicably foiled and rebuffed. Notwithstanding decades of dedicated service as a District of Columbia Public Schools (DCPS) teacher and a plethora of system-acquired and externally acquired credentials, recommendations, and commendations, my career advancement was stymied. I sensed that professional expertise and intellectual acuity, by themselves, were insufficient qualifications for advancement in the school system.

One unfortunate reality was that school principals and central office administrators showed a clear hiring preference for native Washingtonians. Some unofficially justified their preference on the pretext that a native Washingtonian would show greater understanding of and sensitivity to the needs of the students than foreigners or a nonnative Washingtonian educator would. Their argument, though baseless and logically inconsistent, enjoyed expansive currency and credibility in the community and within the school system. As gently and as often as I could, I would counter with the personal question, "If you were gravely sick and had one opportunity for a surgical operation, would you look for the most competent doctor or would you opt uniquely for a native

Washingtonian doctor?" In the final analysis, it was evident that justifying the erroneous argument was more attractive to those benefiting from it. They would rather embrace it than expose the fallacy in it, for to expose the fallacy in it would result in their losing the benefit from it.

With little effort, I realized the immutable presence of a glass ceiling that had, so far, proven impenetrable. For a Sierra Leonean or an African-born male to attain the ranks of school officer, much less gain appointment as a school principal in the District of Columbia Public Schools, was unheard of. I faced the grim reality that it was a feat that no man from Sierra Leone or Africa had ever successfully undertaken in the public school system in the nation's capital. That challenge was the most compelling source of my inspiration and motivation. Even after the dawn of the twenty-first century, it was still normal for school administrators and employing authorities of the school system to echo the encoded refrain, "Under normal circumstances, loyalty cannot be sacrificed for brilliance." The cult-like adherence to this unpublicized but widely embraced credo dictated my fate and restrained my professional advancement. Certainly, several contenders before me had suffered the same fate. Reciprocally, I made it a point of duty never to spare any opportunity to apply for DCPS job vacancies in school administration for which I was qualified.

My determination to forge ahead in spite of the various stumbling blocks remained undiluted. Even after successful interviews, following which some of the interviewers secretly lauded my stellar performance and intellectual acuity, my efforts persisted in being predictably abortive. Year after year, I applied for school administrative positions to no avail. Meanwhile, I participated in multiple system-wide training and internships for school administrators. In addition, I took part in innumerable leadership conferences and presented a variety of professional papers to attain an appreciable level of recognition and respectability among colleagues.

For the time being, these efforts appeared to have yielded nothing of substance. The trend continued unabated while, in addition to my regular teaching assignments, I ungrudgingly but competently performed sundry unscheduled administrative duties at the local school level. Soon, I emerged as a known figure in the prospective pool of the DCPS administrative cadre. In essence, though, neither my strategically aggressive stance nor my unrestrained persistence could halt or reverse the trend. My patience, nearing exhaustion, compelled me to meet with the assistant superintendent to express my disappointment with the selection process. At the conclusion of that meeting, my arguments proved to be both convincing and impressive.

After much toil and following the meeting with the assistant superintendent, I was finally presented with a dubious offer as an assistant principal. That offer, made to me under the expressed threat of possibly (if not probably) being fired within three months, marked the beginning of my journey as a school administrator, assistant principal, and subsequently, a Transformation School principal. That offer presented me with a unique opportunity while exposing me to the serious threat of prematurely terminating my career in education. Thus, I was obliged to excel beyond the need for even the kindest reproach.

Over time, hard work and providence further heaved on me a variety of leadership roles—assistant principal, vice principal, and acting principal. In each of these positions, I demonstrated an enlightened and unwavering insistence on monitoring instruction; improving student safety and school climate; sensitizing teachers and other stakeholders to the needs of students; and improving students' academic performance. That insistence became my watchword and driving force, while students, parents, and educators shared the vision and subscribed to its attainment. In practice, I exemplified a refined devotion to duty and an abundance of professional and personal finesse. As the third year of my tenure as assistant principal slowly elapsed, my efforts showed evident improvement not only in school climate and instructional delivery but also in the conduct and academic performance of students.

With uncommon dedication, I performed my duties with fervency and zeal. Things changed for the better when, on a tranquil summer evening, without notice or premonition, my name popped up on the TV screen in the main office of the school. As my name reappeared on the 6:00 p.m. local TV news, I realized I was among the nine elite school principals who had just been appointed by the new school superintendent to manage nine of the most challenging, underperforming schools in the nation's capital. That local TV announcement marked the beginning of my tenure in the most challenging and most rewarding experience of my life. It summoned me to the task for which I had been preparing for decades; to the opportunities for which I had yearned; to the challenge for self-actualization; and to boldly claim the road less traveled. It was the opportunity for which I had long waited. It validated the sanity in my decision to leave the warmth and comfort of my native land, abdicate the society and institutions that had made me, and—with optimism—confront the endless possibilities of hope. My committing to performing the concomitant moral, civic, and professional duties without evasion or reservation would be the least I could do in return.

My new school, located a couple of blocks from Union Station (a national landmark), was within walking distance of the US Capitol, which houses the US Congress. Transitioning from an assistant principal or vice principal to a principal was extremely time-consuming, mentally challenging, and physically brutal. The demands of a Transformation School further amplified the challenge. Under my tutelage, the school was gradually being transformed to a citadel of learning, where students were constructively engaged academically, where parents felt welcomed, where the community collaborated as partners, and where the faculty and staff felt valued. My school became the most authentic medium for exhibiting my professional preparation, readiness, and stamina. It became the theater where my knowledge, skills, beliefs, attitudes, and character were divulged and where they were all put to the test.

The true test was observed on what started as a peaceful autumn morning in Washington, DC. The school day started like any other, as the students filed into the building, submitted to the usual security check, entered the cafeteria, consumed their breakfast in peace, and visited their lockers before proceeding to their homerooms in preparation for their first-period classes. Halfway into the quasi-hurly-burly of the first period, the school-resource/school-based Metro Police officer dashed into the building and pulled me toward my office. There, he advised me that a total lockdown was to be instituted immediately—New York, Washington, DC, and other US cities were under attack by terrorists. The officer added that the Pentagon had already been struck, and he revealed that airplanes targeting the White House, Union Station, and the Congress were en route. I was jolted by the chilling reality that Union Station, like the Congress and the White House, was within walking distance of the school.

After consultation with my assistant principals, security officers, office staff, counselors, and relevant support staff personnel, I communicated the school lockdown instructions to the faculty. Attempts to reach my immediate supervisor (the assistant superintendent) or any personnel in the school system's central office failed. Equally, efforts to reach my wife, children, and family were abortive. All telephone lines and circuits proved inoperable, and all contacts with locations external to the building were impossible. Isolated and ignorant of any and all emergent external happenings, I focused on maintaining safety and orderliness in the building.

In the school, some of the teachers were poised to exit the building to pick up their children from schools or nurseries or to take their loved ones to or from the hospital. Weighing the needs of the staff against the demands of the school required a delicate balance. The requests of some of the faculty required immediate and positive consideration. At the same time, the safety and security of the students, which was paramount, called for my undivided attention.

Like the teachers and staff, some of the students sought to break loose from school. Some had received text messages from their parents, siblings, or friends, advising them to leave school or report home. Students, like some of the faculty and staff members, were on the verge of taking the law into their own hands, while some parents were banging on several of the dozens of egress doors of the school, demanding entry into the building.

In the building, teachers as well as students were buzzing the school intercom with questions begging for clarification. I was also cognizant that the relative serenity of the building could be easily disturbed by an event as common as a fight among students. Likewise, a lockdown required all building occupants to remain in place without admitting any intruders into the building. Potentially, the balance and equanimity prevalent in the building could be jeopardized by any ill-advised or ill-conceived directive from the school. Meanwhile, I knew that the students could not stay on hold indefinitely. Even without the usual daily supply of fresh bread and milk, the school had to provide lunch for the students present. Likewise, even with reduced staff, the school had to make provisions for bathroom breaks and adequate monitoring and active supervision of students.

With no directive from the Office of the Assistant Superintendent, the local school could not direct the premature closing of school. In the same vein, the local school principal could not summarily dismiss students to unspecified or self-proclaimed surrogates. Additionally, with no school bus in sight, the transportation of students (particularly students with special needs) was fraught with uncertainty.

After consultation with my administrative team, I devised a plan for dismissing students to the designated parent or guardian on file. Also, lunch—consistent with FDA (US Food and Drug Administration) and DCPS guidelines—was served to the students at the usual time and place. By mid afternoon, it was evident that some semblance of normalcy was about to be restored. Communication with the central office was restored that evening, as a good number of parents finally showed up to pick up their children. Arriving home more than fourteen hours after my departure that morning, I felt amply rewarded by the inner strength, resilience, skills, and character that my students, faculty and I had exhibited.

Without a doubt, managing the school during that period of extreme national and local crisis was a balancing act of commitment, courage, and skills. It involved juggling risks, time, space, people, and other varied resources. It showcased the knowledge, skills, and the character acquired and developed over time. The events of 9/11 and the effect on the local school became a bold revelation of the training, commitment, and effective execution of policies, procedures, and practices. The events of that day altered my perception of myself and the world around me. The experience was not only professionally challenging but forever life-altering. My responsibilities that day were among the most professionally challenging of my life. I had to reckon with the enormous demands associated with the gargantuan task of managing a school in the nation's capital. It exposed me to the naked realities of the often-coveted but highly isolated fountain of local school authority. As principal of the school, I was familiar with making decisions with lifelong consequences. However, I never had borne the full weight of making decisions with immediate implications for life or death. It was undoubtedly the tallest order of my avocation.

Losing a Soul Mate among Soulless Mates

This episode narrates the devastating personal loss of Leonora Edith—the physical demise and separation by death of my dearest darling wife, whom, with intimate fondness, I called Leo. Benignly, nature was busy gluing Leo and me together as one, while the unsavory hand of providence was stealthily laying claim to Leo's mortal existence. Sunday, March 28, 2004, some twenty years after my sacred nuptial vow to Leo, was the appointed date of rupture that would forever languish in the dark corner of my mind.

It started a few months after I relocated to the Washington, DC, Metro area. Leo and I first crossed paths on a sunny Sunday afternoon at the Lewisdale residence of a respected Sierra Leonean couple, with whom Leo and I had separately nurtured prior friendships. I was one of many who gathered for a Sunday afternoon barbecue. Then, like a shooting star, my future bride, Leonora, walked in with compelling radiance, beauty, and elegance. She greeted the jubilant gathering one by one. I eyed her and knew then that I would be talking to her in a matter of minutes. As she approached me, I strategically teased her into a conversation, during which I displayed the best I could offer in wit and linguistic brilliance. We soon engaged each other in a profound conversation, at the end of which I affirmed that her exterior beauty, though uniquely exquisite, was by far inferior to the robustness of her internal beauty. By the end of that gathering, I had earned an appointment for the next day. After that first rendezvous, Leo and I were inseparable until the weeks following her hospitalization and subsequent demise. It was ironic that our first appointment was to meet at the Washington Hospital Center, where she was then working and where, coincidentally, I would last see her alive. Outside of my parents and grandparents, Leo was the most influential person in my life and occupied the most coveted corner of my heart.

For twenty years, she oriented my thought processes into accepting the limitless power of prayer, the unconditional love of God, and the unflinching dependence on faith in God. As an ordained Methodist minister, she was consistent in striving to instill in me the grim reality that I was not praying frequently and fervently enough. Even as a professed Christian since birth, I had come to experience, through Leo, the extraordinary power of prayer and the need for a renewed faith in God. During some of the most difficult challenges in our life as husband and wife, when all doors appeared closed and all roads ended, Leo would invoke the mighty power of God, with bended knees and zeal.

Unfailingly, her invocation would open the closed doors and locate hidden exit ramps. With Leo, no problem was too complex for her God and no obstacle too high for her faith. Whether it was the savage turbulence on a transpacific flight to Australia, or the complex meandering of the catacombs of Rome, or walking through a pilfering mob in Caracas, or taking a death-defying boat ride in the shark-infested waters of Martinique, or plying the auto routes of Brussels, or crossing the expansive boulevards of Paris, or driving through the narrow streets of London, or scaling the belly of the Rock of Gibraltar, or taking a late-night walk in the poorly lit streets of Barcelona, Toledo, and Madrid, or venturing into the mazelike Medina of Marrakech, Fez, Casablanca, or Rabat, Leonora was constantly as solid as a rock in her faith in Christ. To allay my fears during some trying moments, she would look at me, sense my trepidation, and say, "Don't worry. I have talked to my Father." Indeed, she was a great woman of God.

In the family, Leo was the unifier. She memorized the telephone numbers of every family member. She would take time out to maintain contact with family members and would urge me to call them as the need arose. Like me, she was as generous with friendliness as she was frugal with friendship. In character, we amply complemented each other.

At home, she was our comforter when the ravages of life yielded nothing but discomfort. She was our most dependable critic and prompter when our memories failed and situations defied logic. Leo was our financial comptroller when deficits loomed, and she was a friend when we were encamped in hostility. Indeed, she was a mother when nurturing and caring were absent in everyone else. Creation offered only one Leonora. She was an irredeemable loss. She was as irreplaceable as she was incomparable. I was yet to be convinced that I could either recover from her demise unscathed or, after her, love again as intensely or as intently. The absence of her caring words, sweet smile, infectious laugh, and gentle touch ceaselessly jolted me to the painful reality that Leonora's earthly mission was over. The lessons learned from her, the gains made with her, and the joys shared with her would remain indelible.

Leo's death forced me to reexamine my purpose in life. It also brought me closer to the realization that our days on earth are numbered and that time is one of humankind's most valuable currencies. The abrupt end to our retirement plans, the uncertainty and often meaninglessness of investment goals, the tenuousness of travel or vacation plans obliged me to reconsider the plausibility of nihilism and the nothingness of humankind. It brought the reality of my mortality to the forefront, as it prepared me for my own demise.

Leo's parting was excruciating. However, more painful than her death was the wicked and ignominious attempts to denigrate her legacy. For different reasons and with sordid motivations, an insignificant minority that claimed to be nearest and dearest to her sought to wreak havoc with their tongues. Like soulless mates, they fueled the flames of discord and turmoil. Using their tongues as weapons of destruction, they selfishly engaged in self-defeating acts of calumny and perfidy. Their desire to steal the limelight (at the expense of the grieving family) led them to squander their integrity and ravage their decency. Like an entity without a soul, they strove to sow turmoil. The stench of some of the insensate lies and innuendos was wicked and overwhelmingly pungent. The sting was unconscionably repulsive, and the weight of the untruth was as brutal as it was disgusting.

Leo left us a legacy that was lofty and unrivaled—examples that were worthy of emulation—and a character that was noble, spirited, and beyond reproach. As her light shines through us, may her soul rest peacefully with the Lord.

Summary

The six life-changing events identified posed the most profound challenges in my life. In addition, these life-changing events bore the potential to be profoundly destabilizing or generously gratifying. Likewise, they provided expanded opportunities for personal growth that could, in turn, lead to social reconstruction. These events caused me to recall James 1:2–8.

> Dear brothers and sisters, whenever trouble comes your way, let it be an opportunity for joy. For when your faith is tested, your endurance has a chance to grow. So let it grow, for when your endurance is fully developed, you will be strong in character and ready for anything.

The events presented potentially destabilizing challenges while constituting a launch pad for greater responsibility and personal growth. I described my six life-changing events primarily for illustrative purposes. They were purely descriptive, not prescriptive. Your own life-changing experiences will differ in essence and intensity.

Like the potter's wheel or the goldsmith's smelting pot, these events created the necessary pressure to alter not only behavior but also character. The events also generated my need for contemplation. In addition, they provided great opportunities for meditation, self-assessment, and self-renewal. In combination with guiding principles that were attuned to all three components of the human triad, these life-changing events, when prayerfully engaged, helped me to construct a favored pathway to peace.

3. Six self-directed maintenance activities to restore and maintain a culture of peace within the context of the guiding principles are as follows:

❖ prayer
❖ fasting
❖ meditation (controlled attention) and contemplation (organized thinking)
❖ trusting
❖ obeying
❖ studying and practicing

The six self-directed maintenance activities provide the third of three legs supporting my quest for peace. They involved providing the tools and resources that would aid my efforts at cultivating and maintaining a culture of peace.

They are maintenance activities that nourish the body, enrich the mind, or fortify the soul. These maintenance activities, in conjunction with the guiding principles, ensure continued and refreshed capacity for peaceful existence that is characterized by self-renewal and self-defined prosperity.

Chapter 5

Guide to Owning and Sowing Peace

The best of people do not begin with
the best of things, but they make the
best of everything they begin.

—author unknown

Concluding the Inconclusive

To maintain peace, we consistently strive to restore peace.
Life's constant stream of peaks and valleys, opportunities
and challenges, joy and sadness are often transported in authentic
experiences and events. The six life-changing events I described
exposed me to life's challenging vicissitudes while equipping

me with the requisite courage, toughness, and ability for a peaceful existence. As important as the life-changing events were, their impact on peace and character formation was largely dependent on the quality of the responses I offered to those situations. The repertoire of options and responses to situations in life is determined by the principles that guide our thoughts and actions. Thus, our responses to life-changing events are constantly filtered through the principles that shape our thoughts and actions. Our guiding principles, therefore, play a pivotal role in determining how we respond to the various situations with which we are confronted.

At the same time, the process of owning and sowing peace is ongoing in the individual, and corporately, it continues ad infinitum. As long as we live, we will be torn between good and evil, life and death, or peace and turmoil. Also, changes will occur in our social environments of people as well as our physical environment of things and ideas. Whether we like it or not and whether we choose to participate in it or not, change will occur. Our world will change, whether we choose to subscribe to the change or not.

Likewise, the pull between peace and turmoil is constant and will continue unabated. Some of us equate life to a restless sea, the waves of which mimic perpetual turmoil and persistent restlessness. The waves of events can be overwhelming and all-consuming at times. So, by its very nature, the road to peace is always under construction. Therefore, the act of owning and sowing seeds of peace is continuous and inconclusive.

Retracing My Path to Peace

My path to peace could be retraced using the three sixes: the guiding principles, the life-changing events, and the maintenance activities.

- The Guiding Principles
  - ❖ Put God first and last; with all human options exhausted, surrender all to Him.
  - ❖ Selflessly show love for God and humankind in all undertakings, while treating others as you want them to treat you.
  - ❖ Ceaselessly and diligently seek to know the world and understand the Word.
  - ❖ Translate knowledge of God and of the world into purpose and actions for daily living.
  - ❖ Show due respect for God, humankind, and all of God's creation, but fear no one.
  - ❖ Subdue improper and irregular passions, and compete with none but self.

In identifying your guiding principles, consider the following:

- o Embrace the understanding that God is always willing and available to lend a helping hand. Therefore, call Him as often as you are able.
- o Build your life and your principles on a solid spiritual foundation.

o   There must be an uncompromised unity of purpose within, between and among the operations of the body, mind, and soul.

o   Read the Bible or book of faith daily.

o   Seek to acquire an accurate and relevant working knowledge of the world.

o   Be kind and generous; never render evil for evil; forgive others, not because they deserve your forgiveness, but because you deserve your peace.

o   Structure your life around a purpose, and let your life be driven by a cause. Allow the purpose to dictate your actions, so that every significant earthly venture is undertaken with a clear purpose that is consistent with your faith.

- Life-Changing Events

The life-changing events or challenges (as may be reflected in your moments of trials and tribulations) are the true test of your spirituality, as well as the true measure of your physical and mental endurance. It is also not uncommon for your greatest accomplishments to be on the other side of the most potentially destabilizing, life-changing challenge.

Remember that life-changing events come in different forms and with varied intensity. As destabilizing as they may be, they serve to toughen you physically and mentally and strengthen you spiritually. They provide genuine rites of passage to spiritual maturity.

Consider the following as you attempt to confront life-changing events:

o   Every adversity is an opportunity with equivalent or greater benefit or gain.

o   Use your mind positively to seek peace. Practice kindness; love and respect everyone. Blame no one, harbor no grudge, and fear no one.

o   Pray fervently; learn from defeat while learning to succeed; engage in meditation (controlled attention) and contemplation (organized thinking) at least twice daily or as your situation warrants.

o   Never downplay the caustic and ungodly power of negative thoughts, words, and attitude.

• The Self-Directed Maintenance Activities

The maintenance activities that are intended and designed to restore and maintain peace follow:

❖ Prayer: Prayer has not only been an open line of communication but also the opening line of my communication with the Lord. I am enjoined to build a prayerful foundation on solid rock. Therefore, I strive to pray like Nehemiah.

❖ Fasting: This prepares me spiritually for intimacy with God. It helps to extinguish or kill the lust of the flesh and subdue self-pride. It compels me to focus attention on the things of God. Fasting and praying conjointly are complementary acts of faith renewal, spiritual purification, and submission to the things of God. To the extent that health conditions permit, I deem fasting once weekly or monthly satisfactory.

❖ Meditation (controlled attention) and contemplation (organized thinking) are to be engaged as David and Moses did. Meditation and contemplation are recommended daily.

❖ Trusting (the unquestioned role of faith and trust, as exemplified by David and Job) is recommended daily and as long and as often as needed.

❖ Obeying (seeking righteousness and obeying uncompromisingly, like Job) is recommended daily and as long and as often as needed.

❖ Studying and practicing the Word and the world (like Timothy) is recommended every day.

General Recommendations

Spiritual and moral awareness is the first step to profound thought, and it is the cradle of informed and godly action. Therefore, establish your guiding principles on a spiritual or godly foundation.

In addition, the guiding principles are to reflect unity among the body, mind, and soul. That is, the function, maintenance, and operations of the body must be achieved in concert with the content and functions of the mind. Therefore, there must be harmony between what the mind conceives and what the body senses or perceives. In this vein, discord results if or when I choose to ingest, inhale, sense, or engage that which the mind repels. Likewise, discord could emanate from a violation that was spiritual in nature. Such a violation could involve a situation and conditions in which activities of the body or the mind are contrary to the dictates and prescriptions from the soul. Such violations would subject us to an uneasy or disturbed conscience and activate personal turmoil. Thus, my pathway to peace could be traced by the consonance within as well as between and among the body, mind, and soul.

To facilitate the attainment of peace, we are to be cognizant of the following statements of caution:

- Self-love begins with loving God first and then loving your neighbor in equal proportion to yourself, for peace rarely exists in the absence of love.
- Focus on loving people and not things. Love empowers people, uplifts us all, and enriches humanity.
- Take time to develop your guiding principles. They connect the three essences of your being and pair you with the dictates of your Creator.
- Be the master of your words, actions, and habits, particularly in matters relating to your body, mind, and soul. Seek righteousness, and obey the Word.
- To experience peace, you must be a force for good and an instrument of peace. Since deceit and lies usually undermine peace, you are to audaciously and lovingly embrace and stand for the truth.

- You cannot start a fight if there is no one to fight. Therefore, to the extent feasible, live peaceably with all individuals.
- Walk away from things that poison your soul.
- Walk away from arguments that debase you or others.
- Walk away from people who aggravate, humiliate, or undervalue your strengths or accentuate your weaknesses.
- Be mindful of the ten characteristics of living a balanced life, by exercising the following (E. Charlesworth and R. Nathan 2004, 368–9):

1. Positive self-awareness: understand where you are coming from.
2. Positive self-esteem: like yourself.
3. Positive self-control: make it happen for yourself.
4. Positive self-motivation: seek to be successful and decide you can.
5. Positive self-expectancy: decide that next time you'll do better.
6. Positive self-image: see yourself changing and growing.
7. Positive self-direction: have a game plan.
8. Positive self-discipline: practice mentally.
9. Positive self-dimension: value yourself as a person.
10. Positive self-projection: reflect yourself in how you walk, listen, and talk.

Bibliography

Achtemeier, Paul J. (Ed) (1985). Harper's Bible dictionary. San Francisco, CA: Harper & Row.

Ahmed, Akbar. (2002). Islam today: A short introduction to the Muslim world. New York, NY. Travis.

Allen, James. (2007). As a man Thinketh. San Diego, CA. Book Tree.

Bak, P. (1996). *How Nature Works.* New York, NY. Copernicus.

Bak, P. & Chen, K. (1991). Self-Organized Criticality, *Scientific American*, January, pp. 46–53.

Beckwith, Michael Bernard. (2008). Spiritual liberation: Fulfilling your soul's potential. Hillsboro, OR. Beyond Words.

Bem, D. (1970). Beliefs, attitudes, and human affairs: Basic concepts in psychological series. Belmont, CA. Brooks/Cole.

Brenner, Frederic. (2003). Diaspora: homelands in exile. New York, NY. Harper Collins.

Brooks, Arthur C. (2008). Gross National Happiness: Why Happiness matters for America. New York, NY. Basic Books.

Charlesworth, E, & Nathan, R. (2004). Stress management: A comprehensive guide. New York, NY. Ballantine.

Chodron, Pema. (2006). Practicing Peace in times of war. Boston, MA. Shambhala.

(The) Columbia Encyclopedia. (2001-09). New York, NY. Columbia University.

Das Surya, Lama. (2007). Buddha is as Buddha does: The ten original practices for enlightened living. New York, NY. Harper Collins.

Emerick, Yahiya. (2004). *Understanding Islam*. New York, NY. Alpha (Penguin Group).

Esposito, J. (2002). What everyone needs to know about Islam. New York, NY. Oxford University Press

Foucher, A. (1963). *The Life of the Buddha*. D. J. and I. CN, Wesleyan University

Goewet, D. J. (2014). The end of stress: Four steps to rewire your brain. Hillsboro, OR. Beyond Words.

Hanh, Thich Nhat. (2003). Creating True Peace: Ending Violence in yourself, your family, your community, and the world. New York, NY. Free Press.

Holmes, T & Rahe, R (1967) The social readjustment rating scales. In: Journal of Psychosomatic research 11: 213-218.

Kalupahana, (1987). *The Way of Disshartha*. MI: University Press.

Maslow, A. H. (1943). <u>A Theory of Human Motivation</u>. *Psychological Review, 50(4)*, 370-396.

Maslow, A. H. (1968). *Toward a Psychology of Being*. New York, NY D. Van Nostrand.

Maslow, A. H. (1970a). *Motivation and personality*. New York, NY. Harper & Row.

Maslow, A., & Lowery, R. (Ed.). (1998). *Toward a psychology of being* (3rd ed.). New York: Wiley & Sons.

Mays, James L. (Ed) (1985) Harper's Bible dictionary. San Francisco, CA. Harper & Row.

McGregor, D. 1960. The human side of enterprise. New York, NY. McGraw Hill.

McLeod, S. A. (2014). Maslow's Hierarchy of Needs. Retrieved from <u>wwww.simplypsychology.org/maslow.html</u>

Mooney, Card Garhart. (2002). Theories of childhood: an introduction to Dewey, Montessori, Erikson, Piaget and Vygotsky.

Nasr, Seyyed Hossein. (2002). The heart of Islam: Enduring values of humanity. New York, NY. Harper San Francisco.

Piaget, J. (2002). The language and thought of the child. New York, NY. Routledge.

Pipher, Mary. (2009). Seeking Peace: Chronicles of the worst Buddhist in the world. New York, NY. Riverhead Books.

Ruiz, D. (1997). The four agreements. San Rafael, CA. Amber-Allen.

Strachey, James (Ed.) (1966). The complete introductory lectures on Psychoanalysis: Sigmund Freud. New York, NY. Norton.

Thomas, E. J. (3d ed. 1960). The Life of Buddha as Legend and History. AC.

Waitley, D. (2004) Empires of the Mind: Lessons to Lead and Succeed in a Knowledge-Based World. New York, NY. Quill

Warmington, E. H. & Rouse, W.H. (Eds) (1956). Great Dialogues of Plato. New York, NY. Mentor

Williams, Montel. (2008). *Living well emotionally: Break through to a life of happiness.* New York, NY. New American Library (NAL).

Born in Freetown, Sierra Leone, Dr. Francis S. Nicol is the fifth of five children born into the union of Lily and Edward Nicol. He attended the Prince of Wales School, then the Milton Margai Teachers College (University of Sierra Leone), and the University of Grenoble, France.

After decades of teaching, coupling the acquisition of six university credentials from four tertiary institutions on three continents, Dr. Nicol was one of nine elite school principals appointed to transform the most challenging underperforming public schools in Washington, DC. He served as school administrator and principal before joining Argosy University faculty, where he served as professor of practice, College of Education.

A national award recipient of the Washington Post Vance Reed Educational Leadership Foundation, George Rogers Fellow, and a Smithsonian Institution National Faculty Fellow, Dr. Nicol participated in educational leadership exchanges to several countries. He has published and presented papers on various topics and public forums. Educational leadership and planning, curriculum, and instruction are among his primary interests. Additionally, he has traveled extensively to more than fifty countries on six continents.

Printed in the United States
By Bookmasters